THE DISPOSABLE WORK FORCE

SOCIAL INSTITUTIONS AND SOCIAL CHANGE

An Aldine de Gruyter Series of Texts and Monographs

EDITED BY

James D. Wright

THE DISPOSABLE WORK FORCE
Worker Displacement and Employment Instability in America

THOMAS S. MOORE

ALDINE DE GRUYTER
New York

About the Author

Thomas S. Moore is a lecturer in the Department of Sociology, University of Wisconsin, Milwaukee. Dr. Moore has written numerous journal articles, and continues to research employment trends and the changing attitudes of American workers.

ALDINE DE GRUYTER
A division of Walter de Gruyter, Inc.
200 Saw Mill River Road
Hawthorne, New York 10532

This publication is printed on acid free paper ∞

Library of Congress Cataloging-in-Publication Data

Moore, Thomas S., 1945–
    The disposable work force : worker displacement and employment instability in America / Thomas S. Moore.
        p. cm. — (Social institutions and social change)
    Includes bibliographical references and index.
    ISBN 0-202-30519-8 (alk. paper) 0-202-30520-1 (paper)
    1. Unemployment—United States. 2. Displaced workers—United States. 3. Full employment policies—United States. 4. Work sharing—United States. 5. Part-time employment—United States. 6. United States—Economic conditions—1981– I. Title. II. Series.
HD5724.M663 1996
331.13'7973—dc20   95-21943
                                                                          CIP

Manufactured in the United States of America

10 9 8 7 6 5 4 3 2 1

To the memory of my parents

Contents

viii   Contents

Preface

This book began as an effort to analyze the local impact of a plant closing against the background of the economic dislocations that are affecting the work force as a whole. As reported in the media, the story of the closing of the Chrysler plant in Kenosha, Wisconsin, and of the community's apparent recovery from that closing impressed me as one-sided and misleading. Many of the news accounts downplayed the hardships experienced by those displaced, but what I found more objectionable was the context in which the story was presented. It was portrayed as an economic development opportunity that benefitted the entire community. There was little or no recognition of the unequal impact that a changing economy and occupational structure are having upon the American work force. This book offers a different perspective. It seeks to link the costs of displacement as they are experienced by individuals within communities to the forces that are reshaping employment relationships throughout society. In the words of C. Wright Mills, I have tried to draw out the connection between "the personal troubles of milieu" and "the public issues of social structure."

The employment trends reported here extend through the early 1990s, but one need only look to the current news headlines for evidence of their continued relevance. As I finish this book, those headlines have just announced that a final round of base closings are projected to result in the loss of 50,000 jobs, a painful reminder of the dislocations that characterize a rapidly changing economy. They also report on the continued sluggishness of wage growth which, after several years of economic expansion, serves as an equally painful reminder of the difficulty that we are having in adjusting to a changing economy. One also need look no further than the news headlines to learn that the Clinton administration's tentative efforts to move toward a more active labor market policy ended with the midterm elections and the Republican takeover in Congress. As funding for educational and job training programs is cut in the name of deficit reduction and for the purpose of tax reduction, the prospect of turning the unemployment system into a reemployment system appears increasingly remote. Nonetheless, the problems that we face are long-term and structural in nature. There appears to be a growing realization that the nature of the employment relationship, and not just the number of new jobs being created, is of fundamental importance to the health of the economy. The quality of employment opportunity is a public issue of social structure, and one that we cannot afford to ignore. My hope is that this book will contribute to a broader discussion of that issue.

* * *

In writing this book I acquired a number of debts that I can only try to repay with a note of thanks. Ken Root was more than generous with his time in reading and commenting on an early draft of the manuscript, and Greg Squires and Ken Meier provided useful advice on how to get the book into print. Thanks are also due to Mike Useem and Richard Koffler for their encouragement and continued interest in a project that I was not sure I would ever finish. Finally, I am indebted to the many students whose not uncritical response to the ideas presented here forced me to clarify my argument. I am afraid that I repaid them by suggesting that their work lives are likely to be more turbulent and insecure than those of their parents.

Introduction:
The Rise of Employment Insecurity ─────────────

> The great risk of downsizing and restructuring is that they'll do nothing to change the way we work. Fewer of us simply will work harder.
> —Keith Hammonds, Kevin Kelly, and Karen Thurston, *Business Week*

The past two decades have witnessed a transformation not only of the organization of work, but also of the opportunities that we have to work and of the terms under which we work. Downsizing, restructuring, outsourcing, these and other buzzwords are invoked to describe the forces that are altering employment relationships throughout the work force. The expectations and obligations that link people to their jobs are changing. Those who tend to view the future in a positive light portray the evolving compact between employer and employee as empowering for the individual. The goal now is lifetime employability based upon continuous learning and skill acquisition; it is no longer lifetime employment based upon loyalty and commitment to the job. Those inclined to a more critical view see a future of growing uncertainty and markedly unequal opportunity. Most people will work longer and harder while millions of others will remain underemployed. Nearly everyone will experience greater job insecurity.

The economic forces transforming our workaday lives are widely recognized and frequently discussed. Technological advance and the heightened competition of a more open world economy are changing a mass production system that once guaranteed a rising standard of living, if not job security, to those it employed. This transformation is most evident in manufacturing, which—like agriculture before it—has experienced an absolute as well as a relative employment decline. But the forces that are reshaping the workplace are being felt in every industry, and they are affecting organizational strategies as well as employment levels. Large corporations are evolving hub and network organizations that better enable them to expand, contract, and relocate employment at will and to impose global market prices upon skilled as well as unskilled workers. More than 20 percent of the output of U.S. firms is produced by foreign workers, and this percentage will increase as companies continue to shift production operations offshore (Reich 1991:120). In a period of low inflation, companies protect profits by cutting labor costs, and the relocation of production facilities abroad is being driven in large part by the search for lower-cost labor.

The search for lower-cost labor does not necessarily mean low-skill labor. Beginning in the late 1970s, U.S. computer companies set up production facilities in India not to employ unskilled workers but to take advantage of a well-trained and relatively inexpensive corps of engineers. The city of Bangalore, the hub of India's Silicon Valley, is now home to over one hundred software and hardware companies, including IBM, Texas Instruments, Hewlett-Packard, and Motorola. The typical engineer in their plants earns about eight hundred dollars a month, a fraction of what a comparably trained worker would make in this country (Gargan 1993). Many service industries too are adapting to a more open world economy by relocating jobs. Metropolitan Life employs 150 workers in a village in County Cork, Ireland, where they examine medical claims from all over the world. The company maintains that these claims examiners are more productive and reliable than their U.S. counterparts. With wages at least 30 percent below those paid here, they are certainly less costly (Barnet 1993). U.S. companies have also increased their research and development spending more rapidly overseas than in this country and now employ accountants, lawyers, engineers, and researchers of every kind in countries around the globe.

The relocation of employment is not all one-sided; foreign-owned companies are investing and creating jobs in this country as well. By 1991 the U.S. affiliates of foreign companies employed approximately 4.8 million workers in this country, double the number they employed in 1981 (U.S. Bureau of the Census 1994:809). Nonetheless, the pressure to shrink corporate work forces and to impose global market prices upon a widening range of occupational skills is resulting in higher rates of job loss. Over the past decade, an average of more than two million people were displaced from their jobs each year. For many, the opportunity for stable, well-paying employment disappeared with their last paycheck. Since 1979 the Fortune 500 companies alone have dismissed over 340,000 workers a year and today employ about 10 percent of the work force, roughly half of their share of employment twenty years ago. This job loss shows no signs of abating. The number of jobs eliminated by these large corporations increased each year of this decade and resulted in the displacement of 615,000 workers in 1993 (Uchitelle 1994).

In addition to cutting employment, more and more companies are outsourcing their noncore operations and relying upon temporary, part-time, and contract employees. The largest private employer in this country is no longer GM or IBM. It is Manpower, Inc., which with 560,000 workers is the world's largest temporary employment agency. Each day Manpower, Inc., and its competitors dispatch one and a half million temporary workers— three times the number of just ten years ago—to offices and factories around the country (Castro 1993). There they join the millions of other contingent workers, including part-timers, independent contractors, and free-lancers, who today make up a quarter of the work force. The advantages to employers of using contingent workers are numerous. Even when these workers are paid at the same wage rates as regular employees, companies reduce their fringe benefit costs and often avoid having to meet equal opportunity and labor standards requirements. There is little reason to fear litigation for unfair labor practices, and little pressure to meet equal opportunity goals, when you never formally hire a large portion of your work force.

A number of trends signal the emergence of a more contingent work force. One of the most obvious is the growing number of involuntary part-time workers. Approximately 18 percent of the work force, more than twenty million people, hold part-time jobs, most of which offer low wages and few benefits. Roughly a quarter of these part-time employees, some five million people, would prefer full-time jobs. Between 1969 and 1989, the proportion of the work force employed part-time increased by 2.6 percentage points, and involuntary part-time workers accounted for two-thirds of this increase (Tilly 1991:10–11). Much of this trend is explained by the shift of employment away from manufacturing to retail trade and service industries. The employment practices of the firms in these industries are often geared to a low-wage, high-turnover labor market made up largely of part-time jobs. There has also been an increase in the use of part-time employment within industries, as firms decide that it is preferable to cut labor costs rather than maintain a stable work force.[1]

Together, widespread job loss and the growing reliance upon contingent labor have reversed a century-long decline in self-employment. Estimates of the number of self-employed vary between twelve and fifteen million, or from 10 to 13 percent of the U.S. work force, depending upon which government agency is doing the estimating. Most are professionals and other traditionally self-employed groups, but some four million are the victims of layoffs, downsizings, and budget cuts. For those who have lost a job it is relatively easy to start a business and become self-employed, but making a comfortable living is considerably more difficult. When economic conditions worsen, the earnings of the self-employed drop sharply.[2] The typical self-employed worker today is part of a large labor reserve that absorbs the decline in earnings during recessions and then provides a flexible labor source as the economy improves.

The economic forces that are undermining the job security of countless workers are also pushing the income distribution toward greater inequality. Over the past two decades, earnings growth has stagnated while earnings inequality has increased. Many of the new jobs being created are in managerial and professional occupations, and this changing occupational mix may have raised the average hourly pay of all workers over the past several

years. However, the real earnings of production and nonsupervisory workers, the majority of the work force, have declined for over twenty years.
These divergent earnings trends are linked to educational differences. As
demand for higher educational skills and credentials has grown, the wage
gap between high school and college graduates has widened. The average
hourly wage for high school graduates fell 12 percent between 1979 and
1991, remained flat for those with a college degree, and rose 8 percent for
those with two years of graduate school.[3] With earnings growth stagnant,
increased earnings inequality has produced a sharp rise in the number of
working poor.

CHANGING EXPECTATIONS

The concept of job security is embedded in cultural assumptions about
what society owes us in return for our labor, and those assumptions are
changing. Few people ever experience a great deal of occupational mobility, but previous generations did aspire to the security of a stable job and a
progressive improvement in their living standards. Company job ladders and
seniority provisions provided both a kind of job security and the promise of
higher earnings. People put in years at a job expecting that performance and
commitment would be rewarded. Today, the constant threat of displacement and the contingent nature of much employment violate this implicit
contract. The expectation that good work will be rewarded with greater job
security is becoming less tenable. As the sense of mutual obligation between
employer and employee breaks down, it alters not only the way that people
feel about their jobs, but also the cultural understandings that sustain a work
ethic.[4] Our understanding of what constitutes good work and of how it
should be rewarded are changing in ways that could undermine the
achievement ethic of less-educated and less-mobile workers.

As the relationship between people and their jobs becomes increasingly
tenuous, the shared experience and social interaction that connect us to
others will also gradually diminish. For some, higher earnings and greater
mobility will compensate for the loss of these nonmaterial rewards. For
others, the work role will simply be less fulfilling. It is little more than a
commonplace to state that work is of fundamental importance for personal
identity. We define who we are and what our place in society is through the
work that we do. Social position and self-concept are inextricably bound up
with the work role. With their work lives disrupted by a rapidly changing
economy and occupational structure, many people risk losing the ability to
demonstrate their worth to others or to define their place in American
society.

These changes in the daily experience of work life and in the stability of
the employment relationship are not simply the reflection of postindustrial

trends. They are also the product of the legal arrangements and rules under which we work. In this country, employers operate within a social and legal environment that only weakly sanctions layoffs and dismissals. Our tax and tariff codes facilitate the movement of production offshore to so-called export processing zones where components can be shipped, assembled, and then reimported duty-free. Our equal-wage laws exempt part-time and temporary workers, and thereby subsidize the growing reliance upon contingent labor. And our national labor laws are weakly enforced, allowing firms to act with impunity in denying collective bargaining rights.

It is this legal environment that accounts for most of the decline in private-sector unions. From a postwar high in 1955 of roughly 35 percent of the nonagricultural labor force, unions today represent no more than 16 percent of the work force and less than 12 percent of private-sector workers. Part of the drop in union membership is explained by shifts in employment from manufacturing to services, and from the more heavily unionized North to the largely nonunion South, but most of the reduction has occurred within industries and regions (Doyle 1985). There has been a marked increase in employer resistance to unionization and a notable weakening of collective bargaining rights. In the 1950s, unions won certification elections for 80 percent of the workers in potential bargaining units and then proceeded to secure contracts for 90 percent of those units. By 1980, unions were winning representations elections for only 40 percent of employees in potential bargaining units and obtained contracts for only half of those units. During this period the proportion of elections in which there were complaints to the National Labor Relations Board about reprisals against union supporters increased threefold, while complaints about bad faith bargaining increased even more rapidly (Weiler 1986:7–8).

One of the more troubling manifestations of the resistance to unions is the growing use of permanent replacement workers to end labor disputes. Companies rarely resorted to this threat before the Reagan administration used permanent replacements to break the 1981 air traffic controllers' strike. Since then an increasing number of companies have employed a tactic that denies any value to stable employment relationships. During the 1992 strike against Caterpillar, a heavy equipment manufacturer, one reporter observed that by threatening to hire permanent replacements the company in effect asserted "that experienced machinists, tool makers and technicians add no more value to the products they make than an untrained job hunter who comes in off the street" (Kilborn 1992).

The decline of employment security affects more than the quality of work life and collective bargaining rights: it also puts the future prosperity of millions of workers at risk. Improvements in worker productivity and earnings increasingly depend upon the continuous learning of new skills. What nobody knows is whether this learning can be sustained as people come to feel more isolated and insecure at work. Employees who are resentful or fearful define their self-interest in narrow and immediate terms. They are not going to invest time and energy acquiring job skills or sharing their insights and ideas when they do not expect to stay at the job. Likewise, employers who view employees as an interim work force are not going to invest in skill development. The level of private investment in worker training in the United States is already low compared to that in most industrial countries. Without a stronger commitment to stable employment relationships, we will continue to underinvest in the human resources upon which our long-term prosperity depends.

OVERVIEW OF THE BOOK

This book examines the downside of the changing employment relationship in the United States. Like all of Gaul, it is divided into three parts. The first part describes the magnitude of worker displacement and the costs and consequences of this job loss. It begins in Chapter 1 with the story of a plant closing and of the efforts of the surrounding community to promote economic growth and recovery. The story of the closing of the Chrysler plant in Kenosha, Wisconsin, illustrates the local impact of economic restructuring and the ways in which communities are adapting to change. By displacing a large fraction of the local work force, the Chrysler closing focused attention upon the costs and benefits of the "public-private partnerships" that promote local economic development. The significance of this plant closing story lies in the issues it raises about the sources of economic growth. Across the country, communities are trying to attract private investment by subsidizing the local costs of doing business. We are trying to attract mobile firms with offers of direct public assistance instead of investing in the skills training upon which our future prosperity depends.

Every plant closing is unique, and the Chrysler closing may not be representative of the dislocations affecting the work force as a whole. Chapter 2 summarizes some of the findings from national labor force surveys and state administrative data regarding worker displacement. It describes the extent of job loss nationwide and its economic costs to the individuals directly affected. On average, more than two million people were displaced from their jobs each year over the past decade, and their lifetime earnings losses were in most cases substantial. For experienced workers, the major economic cost of displacement is a much lower reemployment wage. Chapter 2 also describes how the incidence of displacement and earnings loss shifted between industries and occupational groups during the 1980s. Blue-collar workers continue to bear the brunt of employment change, but white-collar workers are increasingly vulnerable to job loss and economic dislocation.

Both the risks of displacement and its costs have risen for occupational groups that were long sheltered from labor market turbulence.

Chapter 3 identifies the sources of labor market disadvantage that frequently result in lengthy unemployment spells and lower reemployment earnings following a job loss. Among displaced workers, the duration of unemployment spells and the relative wage loss upon reemployment are closely associated, and both can be explained largely within the human capital framework of conventional labor market theory. Individuals with little education or training and those whose skills have become obsolete have greater difficulty finding new jobs and experience proportionately larger wage reductions when they are reemployed. However, not all of the labor market difficulties of displaced workers can be ascribed to educational deficiencies or obsolete skills. The prolonged jobless spells of many experienced workers indicate that there are enduring barriers to effective job search. In addition, the duration of the unemployment spell itself has a negative effect upon job search. The material and psychological deprivations associated with long jobless spells are an obstacle to reemployment for many individuals.

The second part of the book looks at some of the macroeconomic trends—including slower growth, rising earnings and income inequality, and higher average unemployment—that underlie the annual displacement of millions of workers. Chapter 4 examines the productivity slowdown that began in the 1970s. Much of the job loss that is occurring today is blamed upon the declining competitiveness of American industry. The real or imagined loss of competitiveness has become both the explanation and the rationale for moving production offshore, downsizing, cutting domestic wage growth, and eliminating job security provisions. Yet it is not clear what competitiveness means if it does not mean improved productivity and earnings growth. The real threats to competitiveness, and the sources of the productivity slowdown, are internal. They reside in the attitudes and traditional forms of work organization that limit the way in which we are adapting to a new economic environment. They are particularly evident in the failure to invest adequately in our human resources.

Slower economic growth affects the welfare of workers and their families through earnings. Chapter 5 documents the decline in the average real wage and the rise in earnings inequality that can be traced back to the 1970s. Shifts in the supply of educated and experienced workers account for some of the increase in earnings inequality, but the more important factor is the changing nature of labor demand. The earnings opportunities of high school graduates, especially males, have dramatically worsened. The result is not only a less egalitarian society, but also a poorer society. The number of working poor rose over the past decade, and their welfare losses at the bottom of the income distribution outweighed the welfare gains at the top.

The performance of the U.S. economy looks more impressive when we look at the record of employment growth. During the 1970s and 1980s the work force absorbed a larger percentage of the adult population at a time when that population was growing quite rapidly. Despite this job growth, the past two decades witnessed a trend to higher average unemployment. Chapter 6 explains this trend in terms of the longer unemployment spells of traditionally stable labor force groups such as married men. The higher average unemployment of recent years is concentrated among prime-age males who have been displaced and who now remain out of work for longer periods because they cannot find jobs that pay wages comparable to what they once received or to what many similarly qualified workers still receive.

The third and final part of the book argues for a more active public role in regulating the labor market. Contrary to the claims of free-market advocates, an unregulated labor market does not function well. It fails to provide either the information needed to quickly match workers to jobs or the investment in worker training needed to assure future prosperity. Chapter 7 presents the case for a greater training investment in today's workers. It reviews the shortcomings of our public employment and training programs as well as the evidence from state initiatives that follow a more employer-centered approach to training. Employer-centered training offers an alternative to federally funded programs, but it tends to exclude the displaced and disadvantaged workers who most need assistance. Employer-centered programs also tend to subsidize training in skills that are specific to the workplace, training that most firms can be expected to provide in the absence of any public subsidy. To overcome the failings of state and federal programs, we need an employment and training system that gives employers an incentive to invest in the general skills of their employees, an investment that disproportionately benefits less-educated and low-income workers without being targeted exclusively to them.

The argument for a more active labor market policy also rests upon the benefits of employment stability and greater job security. Chapter 8 assesses the possibilities of work sharing as an alternative to temporary layoffs and as a general strategy for combating unemployment. As an alternative to temporary layoffs, work sharing enables firms to adjust to a decline in sales by reducing the average number of hours worked rather than the number of people employed. And public subsidies that lower the cost of short-time work contribute both to labor market flexibility and to employment security. As a strategy for combating unemployment, work sharing calls for reducing the length of the workweek or the workyear in order to create additional jobs. Work sharing proposals that involve mandatory reductions in work time have attracted widespread support in Europe. Similar proposals have generated little interest in this country, but voluntary exchanges of future income for increased time away from the job could eventually reduce the length of the average workyear without lowering current earnings. Work sharing will not eliminate unemployment, but it does represent a collective response to the risk of displacement and to the pervasive sense of economic insecurity.

In a world of global capital flows and rapidly expanding trade, a country's work force is its most valuable asset. Better basic education and opportunities for training throughout the work career are the most effective way to raise earnings and provide greater job security. However, educational reform is a slow process, and there has been little progress in revamping worker training programs. The overhaul of federally funded programs promised by the Clinton administration and its secretary of labor, Robert Reich, is yet to be carried out. Their main accomplishment to date has been a modest reemployment initiative that will streamline the provision of reemployment assistance by establishing one-stop career centers. The goal of turning the unemployment system into a reemployment system remains unrealized. In the meantime, work sharing offers a collective approach to our employment problems. Even modest work sharing initiatives could help to unite a reform coalition.

NOTES

1. Tilly (1991:16) quotes the manager of a health insurance company as explaining, "Our whole drive is to go toward more part-time jobs. It's very cost effective."

2. In inflation-adjusted dollars, the median income for self-employed individuals dropped from a prerecession average of $21,343 in 1989 to $18,815 in 1992 (Uchitelle 1993b).

3. The real hourly wage gains of these educational groups are reported in Greenhouse (1993). The effect of the changing occupational mix upon average earnings over the past several years is reported by Nasar (1994).

4. For a discussion of the impact of worker displacement upon the cultural tradition of opportunity, see Dudley (1994:xv–xxv).

The Costs and Consequences of Worker Displacement

Anatomy of a Plant Closing 1

As a catalyst for ritual communication, a plant closing symbolizes different things to people in different social positions. The Chrysler plant closing dramatized a deep cultural antagonism that has long divided the city of Kenosha.

—Kathryn Dudley, *The End of the Line: Lost Jobs,*
New Lives in Postindustrial America

Plant closings and mass layoffs are unique events, and no single incident is representative of the job loss that is occurring nationwide. But case studies of communities that lose a major employer illustrate some of the trends that are reshaping the employment relationships of millions of Americans. This chapter describes the widely publicized closing of the Chrysler auto assembly plant in Kenosha, Wisconsin.[1] It looks at both the labor market impact of the closing and the efforts of the community to promote economic development and recovery. Those efforts long preceded the Chrysler closing, but they acquired a sense of urgency in the aftermath of the shutdown.

In her study of the Chrysler shutdown, anthropologist Kathryn Dudley (1994) describes how plant closings have come to symbolize change in the economy and the occupational structure. Because of their symbolic importance, they often precipitate a community debate about the meaning of economic change and the sources of communal well-being and future prosperity. As parties to this debate, local elites view plant closings as part of a process of economic development that is ultimately beneficial for the community. For them the Chrysler closing provided an opportunity to assert their belief that the public interest in economic revitalization is best served by reducing the local costs of doing business. The workers directly affected by the job loss are usually more concerned about the unequal costs imposed by plant closings, and they are more likely to question the effectiveness as well as the equity of local economic development initiatives.

Economic development has become the primary focus and substance of local politics in the United States. State and local governments have actively promoted the development of particular locales at least since the 1930s, when southern states began issuing municipal bonds to help finance the construction of industrial plants. The issuance of tax-free bonds to reduce the borrowing costs of private firms has since evolved into "public-private partnerships" through which state and local governments offer a wide variety of financial incentives to attract private investment. There is little evidence that subsidizing private firms reduces the long-term unemployment rate or improves the employment prospects of local residents, but the prevailing approach to economic development emphasizes boosterism and business investment incentives as the way to attract companies and jobs to hard-pressed communities. And communities that lose their major industrial employer are certainly hard-pressed.

THE EVENTS LEADING UP TO THE CLOSING

Kenosha's main assembly plant had been used to produce cars since 1902, when a local businessman, Thomas P. Jeffrey, began building Ramblers in what had been a bicycle factory. At the time of the closing in December 1988, it was the oldest operating car assembly plant in North America. The community's employment and income levels had been highly unstable for decades, both because of the cyclical nature of the auto industry and because Chrysler's predecessor, the American Motors Corporation (AMC), held only a small and declining share of the domestic car market. But when Chrysler purchased AMC in the summer of 1987 and spent millions of dollars to retrofit the old plant for assembly of its Dodge Omni and Plymouth Horizon subcompacts, it reassured residents that auto production would continue. Expectations soared when thousands of laid-off workers were recalled, and many left full-time jobs to return to what they were assured was a renovated plant.

Those expectations were shared by the state and local officials who made every effort to accommodate the carmaker's demands for public assistance, including job retraining funds, infrastructural improvements, a thirty-million-dollar state loan financed at below-market rates by the sale of government bonds, and the assignment to Chrysler of up to four thousand tons of the state's allotted emissions of volatile organic compounds. The provision of this emission allotment is indicative of the importance that states and localities attach to keeping major employers. Southeastern Wisconsin has poor air quality and is classified as a nonattainment area by the Environmental Protection Agency. By granting such a large portion of its emissions credits to Chrysler, the state effectively limited the expansion or entry to the area of other industrial firms.

In return for acceding to Chrysler's demands, Wisconsin officials received assurances that car production would continue through the 1992 model year. In a letter to the Kenosha city administrator dated July 26, 1987, Chrysler's manager of state relations, James Kilroy, recalled the promises he had made at an earlier meeting with the Kenosha Common Council and stated,

Based upon our current production plans, it is our intention to maintain production of our L-body vehicles for at least five years in the American Motors facilities located in your city.[2]

Despite this assurance, it became increasingly clear during the fall of 1987 that Chrysler's intentions had changed and that it was planning to close the plant. By acquiring AMC, the company had raised its break-even point in annual vehicle sales at a time of growing overcapacity and intense competition in the domestic car market. Its Kenosha work force had an exceptional quality control record, but the antiquated facility imposed production costs well above the company average. Lowering those costs would have required substantial new construction, and Chrysler was already committed to rebuilding its Jefferson Avenue plant in Detroit. In a clear signal of its true intent, Chrysler refused to negotiate a written agreement with the state's Department of Development that would have allowed disbursement of the job retraining funds demanded just months earlier.

Disregarding this and other warnings, the state's Republican governor, Tommy Thompson, continued to exude what one Democratic lawmaker later termed an "inflated optimism." Since winning the governorship in 1986, Thompson had cultivated a political image as Wisconsin's biggest economic development booster, and he kept his dealings with Chrysler private, involving neither the Democratic-controlled legislature nor the union. This strategy fueled accusations that he was playing "Lone Ranger" in order to take political credit for the state's economic development efforts. Those efforts were now highly politicized, and he faced the risk of being blamed for an economic development failure. That risk became reality on January 27, 1988, when Chrysler announced that it would close the assembly plant by the end of the year, leaving some 5,500 employees, or half of the city's industrial work force, without a job.

Reenacting a drama that has played across the country, area residents responded to the announcement with a mixture of anger and dismay. The loss of so many well-paying jobs threatened hardship both for the workers and families directly affected by the closing and for those whose livelihoods depended, one way or another, upon the income that auto production brought into the community. The depth of the resentment over what was perceived as a betrayal of trust was not hard to gauge. Within weeks the largest labor rally seen in southeastern Wisconsin in years gathered to hear Jesse Jackson denounce the closing, union members began picketing Chrysler meetings and press conferences, and the state assembly voted ninety to two to ask Chrysler to honor its commitments to the people of Wisconsin. Reflecting the feelings of their constituents, the state's congressional delegation, led by Kenosha's representative Les Aspin, pointed out in a letter to Chrysler's chairman, Lee Iacocca, that the company had asked for and received substantial public assistance in return for agreeing to keep the plant open for five years. Perhaps the most telling indicator of community feeling was the tavern sign across from the main Kenosha plant. Following the closing announcement its message was changed from "Lee Iacocca for President" to "Lee Iacocca Lied to Us."

Disappointed to learn that the plant would shut down, a number of public officials called upon the state to file a lawsuit against Chrysler. Among those threatening legal action was Governor Thompson, who declared at a meeting with the Chrysler workers,

> I'm darn serious about the lawsuit. It's not a threat, I'm not afraid of filing a lawsuit. It's not going to hurt business. If businesses can't keep their word, we don't want them in Wisconsin. (*Racine Labor* 1988)

Surprised and politically embarrassed by the announced closing, and not wanting to become a target of the anger it aroused, Thompson sought to focus attention upon the apparent duplicity of Chrysler while presenting himself as the state's chief prosecutor of corporate wrongdoing. Declaring himself disgusted, he vowed to sue Chrysler either to keep the plant open or to pay one hundred million dollars in damages. He also responded to the charge that he had been naive in his dealings with Chrysler by directing the state attorney general to release three hundred pages of documents that, along with the company's oral assurances, supposedly proved that it was legally obligated to continue assembly operations in Kenosha. Whether a court would have agreed that a contractual obligation existed is debatable, but the threat probably got the attention of Chrysler's lawyers.[3] It certainly shored up the governor's political image. A telephone poll of state residents in February revealed that 61 percent favored a lawsuit and that Thompson's approval rating had not changed while that of Iacocca had plummeted (*Milwaukee Journal* 1988).

Chrysler officials were clearly surprised by the extent and the tone of the publicity generated by the closing announcement. Iacocca's image as a straight-talking man of the people was being tarnished, and he tried to defuse the situation by becoming personally involved. In a strikingly candid admission of the company's miscalculation, if not mismanagement, the Chrysler chairman stated, "We are guilty of being cock-eyed optimists. . . . Blame us for being dumb managers, but don't call me a liar" (White 1988a). Iacocca also promised to repay any money that the city and county of Kenosha had spent on the Chrysler facilities and announced the creation of a twenty-million-dollar trust fund for the Kenosha workers to be financed from the company's 1988 Wisconsin sales. Although well received, this trust fund was motivated by more than a sense of moral obligation to help. Chrysler's sales had dropped sharply within a one-hundred-mile radius of Kenosha, and tying layoff aid to sales improved both the corporate image and the sales of its Wisconsin dealers. Most importantly, the favorable publicity given the trust fund eroded support for legal action against Chrysler, which was undoubtedly the intended effect of the offer.

Following the public rally in early February, the auto workers' union, UAW Local 72, initiated a campaign to mobilize public opinion, hoping to force Chrysler to honor its commitment and keep the plant open. As part of that campaign, the union local also prepared to file suit against Chrysler for using fifty million dollars in federal grants to retool its Detroit facilities for production of the Omni and Horizon subcompacts. The use of federal funds for the purpose of relocating plants and/or jobs is prohibited, and Chrysler claimed that the federal monies it received were being used to construct a new plant, not to retrofit the older plant to which production was being shifted. This accounting practice may have been legal, but the threatened suit served as a bargaining chip in the union's negotiations with the company. In late April, Chrysler reached agreement with the union on pension and severance benefits and guaranteed that the engine plant in Kenosha would remain open for at least five years. In return, the union dropped its lawsuit.

At the time, union members hoped that the legal actions threatened by state and local officials would prevent or further delay the closing. Both the Kenosha city council and the county board had voted unanimously to pursue every legal option to keep the plant open, and the governor had publicly supported a breach-of-contract suit against Chrysler. However, during the months following the closing announcement, prominent business leaders and organizations became increasingly vocal in criticizing the proposed lawsuit as injurious to the state's investment climate. Within Kenosha, the Manufacturers' Association, the Chamber of Commerce, and the Kenosha Area Development Corporation all urged the city council and the county board to oppose the suit. The pressure on local lawmakers increased as it became clear to Thompson that public concern over the closing was diminishing. The governor was anxious to resume his role as the state's major business booster, and he needed to diffuse responsibility for a settlement with Chrysler that would amount, in essence, to dropping the lawsuit.

At a public town hall meeting on September 22, the Kenosha city council voted fourteen to three and the county board voted nineteen to three, with three abstentions, to accept a plant-closing deal offered by Chrysler. The hundreds of Chrysler workers who attended the meeting were outraged by what they regarded as a sellout, and most of the politicians had to be escorted out of the meeting hall by police. Many later defended their action by claiming that representatives of Governor Thompson and of Congressman Aspin had argued that the area's future economic development would be jeopardized if they proceeded with the suit. They voted for the settlement to avoid being labeled antibusiness and to put the plant closing behind them.

The following day Thompson signed an agreement with Chrysler. The press release outlining the terms of the agreement pointed to its endorsement by the local lawmakers and claimed that the settlement was the best attainable. In the press release, the governor's office also took credit for the far more substantial concessions that had already been won by the union, even though the settlement between Chrysler and the State of Wisconsin actually amounted to about six million dollars in additional grants and loans. With this agreement to drop the breach-of-contract suit, the effort to keep the state's largest industrial employer ceased. On December 23, 1988, the final car rolled off the Kenosha assembly line, bringing an end to eighty-six years of auto production.

Community leaders had long anticipated the end of auto production in Kenosha and had urged diversification of the local economy. But the timing of the closing announcement, coming as it did after assurances that assembly operations would continue, came as a surprise to residents and as an embarrassment to public officials. Their anger was genuine. Whether or not the closing could have been avoided, the way in which the decision was reached caused needless hardship. It is conceivable that Chrysler management misread the market in recalling thousands of laid-off workers and assuring the community of their intention to keep the plant open. It is possible that they were just dumb managers, as Iacocca claimed. But it is more likely that they viewed the Kenosha plant as a pawn in the collective-bargaining game. Chrysler's purchase of AMC was motivated by its desire to obtain the four-wheel-drive Jeep line that was produced in Toledo, Ohio. Continuing production in Kenosha provided an option, and a threat, during contract negotiations with the union local in Toledo. Had those negotiations broken off, the production of the popular Jeep vehicle could have been transferred to Kenosha. If Chrysler executives misjudged anything, they misjudged the repercussions of playing off one work force against another, and one community against another, as part of a bargaining strategy.

The use of boosterism as a form of partisan politics also contributed to the misunderstanding and ill will generated by the closing. In keeping his dealings with Chrysler private, Wisconsin's governor sought personal credit and partisan advantage from investment decisions over which he had little influence. He badly misread Chrysler's intentions and then, seeking to avoid political blame, proclaimed a contractual obligation that he was not willing to enforce. Overly trusting in his dealings with a major corporate actor, he proved considerably more adept at managing public perceptions and at influencing the actions of local officials.

THE AFTERMATH OF THE CLOSING: TWO TALES OF A CITY

Neither Chrysler's executives nor the governor personally had to bear the economic costs of the shutdown. The immediate impact of any plant closing is borne by the workers displaced from their jobs and by their families. Through their lives the effects of the shutdown ripple through the labor market and the larger community. In Kenosha this impact was mitigated somewhat by the early retirement, at a reduced benefits level, of over one thousand workers and by the relatively favorable settlement negotiated by the union. Still, the Chrysler closing cost the community an annual payroll of at least $130 million, the loss of over a million dollars a year in city property taxes, and large reductions in local utility revenues. It also disrupted the lives of thousands of individuals.

No government agency in this country tracks the employment histories of workers displaced by plant closings, and precise figures on the reemployment status of the Chrysler workers are not available. In March 1990, fifteen months after the shutdown, more than three thousand laid-off workers were still registered with the state employment service (Wisconsin Job Service 1990). The difficulty most workers experienced finding new jobs was also evident in the unexpected response to the voluntary reemployment training program conducted at the Displaced Workers' Center in Kenosha. By March 1990, a total of 2,894 former workers had enrolled in the program, with only 966 placed in unsubsidized jobs (Ward 1990). Excluding those who took early retirement, it appears that well over half of the Chrysler workers remained jobless for more than a year.

County employment and earnings data collected by the Wisconsin Job Service document the impact of the closing upon the local labor market.[4] In December 1988, immediately prior to the closing, 54,200 people were employed in Kenosha County and the unemployment rate was 3.4 percent. One year later, 49,800 were working and unemployment had jumped to 6.4 percent. The unemployment figure did not increase as dramatically as expected because many workers dropped out of the labor force. The county labor force decreased by 3,000 workers in the year following the closing and did not regain its 1988 level until three years later. The downward shift in the area wage distribution was just as precipitous and was more long lasting. From $13.02 an hour in 1988, the average real production wage dropped 10 to 15 percent and was still below its 1988 level five years after the closing. The earnings ability of the average production worker declined appreciably. Together, the smaller number of wage earners and the lower average wage level reduced the county's private-sector payroll from $197 million in the final quarter of 1988 to $166 million in the final quarter of 1989, a decrease of nearly 16 percent. The community's income stream has increased in the years since, but many local businesses and community agencies were adversely affected by the drop-off. The impact upon local charities was especially severe. In 1987–88 Chrysler employees donated $385,000 to the Kenosha United Way. The following year they gave $40,000, forcing funding cuts of as much as 35 percent for the twenty-eight member agencies (Soukup 1988).

The loss of thousands of well-paying blue-collar jobs also exacerbated family income inequalities and contributed to the economic difficulties of the area's minority community. In Kenosha as elsewhere, minority workers are more likely to be displaced; once displaced, they have considerably greater difficulty finding new jobs at comparable wage rates (Moore 1992). Blacks and Hispanics make up about 9 percent of the labor force in southeast Wisconsin, but they represented 21 percent of the former Chrysler workers registered with the state employment service fifteen months after the closing (Wisconsin Job Service 1990). The editor of a local labor newspaper commented upon the significance of these employment figures:

> There are some incredible social crises taking place in the black communities in the industrial cities of Kenosha, Racine, and Milwaukee . . . [and] they are directly tied to deindustrialization. There is a lot of talk about the creation of the black underclass by the welfare state. . . . In fact, there has been a destruction of the black working class by the decisions of corporations like Chrysler.[5]

* * * *

Most accounts of Kenosha's economic recovery portray it in a very positive light, despite the hardships imposed by the plant closing. When it became clear that the Chrysler pullout was unavoidable, public officials and business leaders sought to focus attention upon the growth sectors of the local economy and upon their efforts to promote the area to potential investors. Those efforts were coordinated through the Kenosha Area Development Corporation (KADC), a public-private partnership created in 1983 to help local businesses and relocating firms obtain various forms of financial assistance. Stories of the development initiatives spearheaded by KADC became a regular feature in the local media: Projecting a growth-oriented image of the community, the local newspaper even began referring to Kenosha as "Boom County."

In interviews conducted during the year following the closing, many business and community leaders expressed their belief that the community was recovering rapidly and that the promotional efforts of KADC were largely responsible for the recovery.[6] One prominent business leader stated, "When I first came here, we were not really doing anything to invite anyone to come here. Now we are inviting and people are accepting our invitations." Asked if the city's economic prospects were better or worse than they were ten years ago, several respondents echoed the sentiments of the local public official who answered, "Substantially better, dramatically better, they have never been better."

These respondents obviously regarded the Chrysler closing as a positive development for the community as a whole. Their views may express a desire to put the closing behind them, but they also reflected their vision of the city's future. Many believed that the shutdown had removed the major obstacles to economic development: the Chrysler wage scale and the presence of a powerful union local. As one local development official stated with unusual candor,

> I think the perception of Kenosha was a militant labor town and to locate here you had to be union and pay sixteen dollars per hour. . . . The dominance of the Chrysler wage scale has not been eliminated, but it has been minimized.

Asked about Kenosha's selling points, he added, "Higher unemployment gives us a definite market advantage." This viewpoint was shared by other officials who noted that "high unemployment makes for no shortage of workers" and that the closing "signaled people who had been reluctant to invest an opportunity to come in and invest."

Kenosha is attracting new investment, but neither the Chrysler closing nor the promotional efforts and incentives offered through KADC are the primary reason for its economic recovery. The basis of its locational advantage is geography. The city lies on the shore of Lake Michigan midway between Chicago and Milwaukee, to which it is linked by two rail lines, a port, and an interstate highway. This central location attracted an in-migration of new residents and businesses long before the Chrysler closing made economic development the focus of public attention. Housing and overall living costs are substantially lower than they are in adjoining Lake County, Illinois, and the area is home to a growing number of Illinois commuters. The president of the local real estate association has estimated that, depending on location, 30 to 60 percent of home sales are to Illinois residents (*Kenosha News* 1990). The growing housing demand has raised local property values and fueled a building boom.

The same locational advantage accounts for the construction of industrial parks and the relocation of transportation and warehousing operations to the area. Industrial park land is either unavailable or prohibitively expensive in neighboring Lake County, and the city's fourteen-hundred-acre LakeView Corporate Park is attracting firms to the area. LakeView will generate tax revenues for years to come and has already raised land values, but it has produced few new jobs. When development began in 1988, it was expected that the park would create thirty-nine thousand new jobs. By 1993, twenty-eight companies employing 2,658 people had moved into the park. A majority of these companies are transplants, and many have relocated from Illinois, bringing their former employees with them (Sharma-Jenson 1993).

Kenosha's location near the center of the nation's third largest population agglomeration also makes it attractive for commercial and recreational development. Drawn by the large traffic volume and the escalating land values, a growing number of factory retail outlets and a greyhound racing track are located along the interstate. With ten million people living within seventy-five miles and with dog racing illegal in Illinois, it was a pretty safe bet that the track would draw visitors to the area. Within days of voting to drop the breach-of-contract suit against Chrysler, the Kenosha Common Council also approved a multimillion-dollar bond to begin construction of a marina in hopes that it would rejuvenate a lake front long dominated by Chrysler's assembly plant.[7] The marina has not drawn thousands of visitors, but it was expected to rent most of its boat slips to Illinois residents.

Because of its favorable geographic location, Kenosha has weathered the loss of its major employer. Increased commercial activity and the in-migration of white-collar residents and commuters have raised per capita income and created a housing boom. One conservative commentator, writing in the Heritage Foundation's *Policy Review*, even characterized the community as "a testament to the resiliency of market capitalism, traditional values, and conservative economic policies" (Glass 1994). Such tributes notwithstanding, Kenosha remains a very divided community, and the benefits of its economic recovery have not been equally shared. Since local residents ultimately bear the costs of economic growth, the question of who benefits from that growth is one of equity as well as of market efficiency.

LOCAL ECONOMIC DEVELOPMENT: WHO BENEFITS?

Kenosha is typical of American communities in the extent to which economic development has become the primary responsibility and preoccupation of local public officials. The separation of powers inherent in our federal system gives state and local government the autonomy to pursue their own development policies, while at the same time restricting national policy initiatives. Kenosha is also typical of the way in which most communities pursue economic growth. Within the public-private partnerships that promote local development, the primary responsibility of government is to influence private investment decisions by reducing the local cost of doing business (Eisinger 1988). By offering incentives that lower the price of land, labor, and capital, state and local governments seek to create a locational advantage that will attract new investment and spur economic growth.

Virtually every state and many cities now support their own economic development agencies at considerable cost to taxpayers. In 1990 state development agencies alone spent one and one-half billion dollars on programs that directly assist business and budgeted an additional five hundred million dollars to support high-technology development (Bartik 1990:6–7). These expenditures are dwarfed by the value of off-budget subsidies such as property tax abatements, tax-free financing, and business tax reductions. The total cost of these subsidies is not known, but they represent a huge revenue loss that forces states and localities either to shift the tax burden onto individual taxpayers or to cut back on services.

This revenue loss is the inevitable result of the competition to attract private firms by means of locational incentives, a competition that has come to resemble what game theorists term the *prisoner's dilemma*.[8] Like prisoners charged with the same crime but separately offered a plea bargain, it is in the interest of each state or locality to grant mobile firms a favorable deal before one of their neighbors does. The result of this beggar-thy-neighbor competition is that states and localities lose billions of dollars of potential revenue and end up collectively worse off. The dilemma is that an individual state or locality cannot afford to stop bargaining. When Michigan tried to end the bidding wars by getting the other states in its region to agree to stop offering local property tax breaks as incentives, the offer was rejected (*Economist* 1989).

Communities that seek to attract private investment with tax breaks and business subsidies incur both direct costs and even larger revenue losses. Even though the total value of these locational incentives is large, their value to individual firms represents a small portion of total production costs: too small in the opinion of their critics to influence most business location decisions. The tax breaks and subsidies given to Chrysler did not influence its decisions to acquire AMC or subsequently to close the Kenosha plant, and the movement of other firms into the area is a tribute to the advantages of geographic location more than anything else. The proponents of business incentives argue that lowering the local cost of doing business results in greater investment than would otherwise occur, and a number of studies have found that general tax reductions are associated with increased business activity (Bartik 1990:36–44). However, the long-run impact of any tax reduction depends upon the ability and willingness of local residents to make up the lost revenue. In cases where the tax burden cannot be shifted and revenues drop, the eventual deterioration in government services and infrastructure will likely discourage future investment and negate the advantage of lower tax rates. At best, locational incentives stimulate business activity at the cost of a redistribution of the tax burden. Often they amount to business giveaways that eventually detract from the quality of life within a community.

The most important claim made in defense of business subsidies is that they benefit local residents by stimulating economic growth and creating new and better employment opportunities. Faster-than-average growth can lower the unemployment rate and raise wage levels in the short run. Even a temporary increase in labor demand creates job opportunities as employers either raise wage rates or relax hiring standards and take on employees who they would not have hired previously. Over the longer term, in-migration tends to erase these gains. The number of job-seekers migrating between areas is always much larger than local differences in the number of jobs being created, so local unemployment and wage levels will quickly return to the regional average (Marston 1985). Whether local job-seekers have the opportunity to gain experience and to acquire skills that increase their future earnings depends upon the kind of jobs made available. Where local employment growth takes the form of low-wage, low-skill jobs, and where higher-skill jobs are filled by in-migrants, business expansion will have little effect upon the unemployment rate or the earnings ability of long-term residents. It will have a much greater effect upon land values. Unlike labor, land cannot migrate into an area to force prices down. Local economic growth permanently raises land values and principally benefits land-owning elites (Logan and Molotch 1987). Thus while the competition to attract mobile capital improves the employment prospects of residents temporarily, if at all, it confers lasting benefits upon real estate and commercial interests.

Kenosha's economy is creating new jobs, but much of the job growth is concentrated in the low-wage retail sales and service sectors. And although the local work force is growing, the wages of production workers remain depressed. Most of the companies locating in the industrial park pay high wages, but they employ relatively few people, many of whom relocated along with their jobs. Meanwhile, long-time residents are discovering that the rising land values that benefit real estate, construction, and commercial interests mean higher housing costs and increased property taxes. Despite its locational advantages, Kenosha's economic recovery is being accompanied by growing social inequality.

RETHINKING ECONOMIC DEVELOPMENT

Across the country, communities threatened with plant closings and lay-offs are offering financial incentives in an effort to influence the investment decisions of private firms. The competition to attract and retain mobile capital results in the loss of potential revenue and either shifts the tax burden onto local residents or forces cutbacks in government services and public investment. Nationwide, the competition is more likely to redistribute existing jobs than it is to create new ones, and it has little or no effect upon the unemployment rate. As long as efforts to attract mobile firms simply transfer jobs from one locality to another without increasing the total number of jobs, business subsidies and tax breaks will lower unemployment in one area only by raising it in another.[9] The communities such as Kenosha that do attract new investment often find that their economic recovery is uneven. Selected economic sectors and occupational groups prosper, but real estate and recreational developments, commercial expansion, and even the capturing of a few industrial firms do not improve the earnings ability of most area residents.

The greatest failing of the traditional approach to development is that it misconstrues the meaning of economic growth and thereby limits our ability to pursue alternative policies. The notion of comparative locational advantage based upon the relative costs of land, labor, and capital becomes the sole criterion by which public initiatives are judged. The crucial importance of worker productivity and skill development is overshadowed by the effort to reduce wage rates, and economic welfare is measured by the number of jobs created rather than by the earnings that those jobs generate.

An alternative approach to community development emphasizes new capital formation. It rejects the idea that lower wages and the competition to attract existing firms are the keys to economic growth. Growth increasingly depends upon the ability to exploit new markets, and state and local government can play an active role in that process. The role of government should be to reduce risk and to help local companies develop new markets by generating venture capital, supporting high-tech research and development, and promoting export goods (Eisinger 1988:7–12). This approach would not preclude offering tax breaks and subsidies to private firms, but it would make all such assistance conditional upon their willingness to meet specific public goals, such as the hiring and training of local workers.

Developing new markets and promoting technological innovation are necessary, but they are not sufficient to assure long-term earnings growth. We also need to invest in work-based learning. We confront young people with what is perhaps the most difficult school-to-work transition in any major industrial country, and we systematically underinvest in worker training and skill development. These problems need to be addressed at the national level, but their solution ultimately depends upon our willingness to rethink what community development really means. Without a commitment to raising the earnings ability of the average worker, local development efforts will only reinforce and magnify the social divisions within our communities and nation.

The critical point in the drama of the Chrysler closing came on the September evening when the city council and the county board voted to drop the lawsuit. In the minds of most of these local politicians, it was a vote for economic revitalization. But they were also voting for an economic and social reorganization of the community that left little place for its blue-collar work force. Kathryn Dudley quotes a city council member who voted against dropping the lawsuit:

They really don't give a damn about a lot of these people. [Blue-collar voters] didn't support them, you know, so it's no big deal to them. They'd like them out of town. They'd like to bring in a lot of people from the suburbs of Chicago, repopulate large parts of the city, and make it a yuppie bedroom community. That's what they would really like to do. (1994:69)

The issue here is not the outcome of the vote; it is this vision of the city's future. It assumes that we can transform our communities by subsidizing private development, while encouraging those displaced in the process to just go away. A more equitable and a more realistic vision would link the future prosperity of both community and nation to the earnings ability of those adversely affected by economic change.

NOTES

1.   The account of the Chrysler shutdown presented here draws upon Moore and Squires (1991).
2.   Kilroy's letter was among the documents that the state made public after the closing announcement.
3.   Inspiration for the state's lawsuit came from West Virginia's breach-of-contract suit against the Newell Corporation. That suit is cited for the innovative principle of forcing companies that accept subsidies to compensate the communities they leave (see White 1988b).
4.   County employment and earnings figures are from the Wisconsin Job Service's *Employment Review* (see Moore and Squires 1991:167–68).
5.   Local business and community leaders were interviewed during the year following the Chrysler closing as part of a study of the city's economic development efforts. The format and findings of the interviews are discussed in Moore and Squires (1991).
6.   Although most of these respondents viewed the closing as a positive development, there was sharp disagreement regarding its long-term impact upon the community, as the preceding quote shows.
7.   The new marina is symbolic of the city's physical and social transformation (Dudley 1994). Ironically, the project recently required a financial bailout to avoid defaulting on its debt.
8.   In the classic plea-bargaining situation involving two prisoners, each suspect is separately offered a reduced sentence for incriminating the other. The rational course of action for each individual prisoner is to make a deal even though the combined sentence is greater than it would be if they both refused to bargain.
9.   It is theoretically possible for investment subsidies to relax the macroeconomic constraints upon employment, but there is no evidence that locational incentives result in net job growth nationwide (see Bartik 1990:196–99).

The Magnitude and Costs of Worker Displacement 2

One implication of our findings is that existing government programs do not, and probably cannot, compensate for more than a small portion of displaced workers' losses.

—Louis Jacobson, Robert LaLonde, and Daniel Sullivan,
The Costs of Worker Dislocation

Factory closings and mass layoffs have come to symbolize a changing economy and occupational structure. Case studies of closings such as the Chrysler shutdown reveal the labor market impact of large-scale job loss: its effects upon the individuals displaced and the larger community. Just as importantly, they show how communities are adapting to economic change. But plant closings account for only a portion of job loss, and case studies cannot measure the extent of displacement nationwide or the magnitude of its costs.

These limitations have led researchers to look to national labor force surveys for information on what is usually a small subsample of displaced workers. Given the difficulty of measuring the extent of job loss with surveys that were not designed for that purpose, the Bureau of Labor Statistics (BLS) commissioned the Census Bureau to add a series of questions for displaced workers to the *Current Population Survey* (CPS). The latter is the household survey that provides monthly unemployment statistics and, as such, is uniquely suited to measuring the extent of job loss. Beginning in January 1984, and since repeated at two-year intervals, respondents from the approximately sixty thousand households in the CPS were asked whether any adult member had lost a job during the preceding five-year period. If the answer was yes, they were then questioned about the nature of the former job and their subsequent (un)employment experience. In the years since its initial installment, these *Displaced Worker Surveys* (DWS) have become the primary source of information on the extent of displacement within the American work force.

This chapter describes the changing profile of the displaced population as seen through the biennial DWS. It documents the extent of worker displacement during the ten-year period from 1982 to 1991. It also looks at the changing incidence of job loss across industries and occupations and among different labor force groups. During this period, the rate of job loss decreased in manufacturing and increased in major service industries, and the displaced work force represents an increasingly diverse range of industries and occupations as a result. The incidence of job loss is still higher among younger and less-educated individuals, and among production and non-supervisory workers. White-collar occupations continue to offer relatively stable employment, but as the industry location of job loss has shifted, the risk of displacement for well-educated, white-collar workers has increased.

Measuring the rate of worker displacement is relatively straightforward. Assessing its economic costs is much more difficult. The DWS was not designed to measure the earnings of displaced workers over time, and the best estimates of their total earnings loss are derived from state administrative data. Although the DWS does not accurately measure the amount of earnings loss, it does allow us to compare the percentage wage reductions among different work force groups. That comparison indicates that the economic costs of displacement were greater in 1990–91 than in the earlier recessionary period of 1982–83 and that these costs have risen among college-educated and white-collar workers. Middle-class anxieties over the incidence and costs of job loss have some basis in fact. The threat of economic dislocation and downward mobility has grown for many occupational groups.

WHO ARE DISPLACED WORKERS?

Estimates of the size of the displaced work force vary greatly depending upon how we define displacement, and there is no general agreement upon the precise meaning of that term. Some researchers view displacement as synonymous with dislocation and attempt to identify only those job losers who are likely to have trouble finding comparable employment (e.g., Browne 1985). Aside from the difficulty of determining, at the time of job loss, which workers will experience reemployment problems, this approach begs the question of what the consequences of displacement are.[1] The goal of most studies is to measure the duration of the unemployment spells and the magnitude of the earnings reductions associated with job loss. These negative outcomes are the object of inquiry, but they do not define displacement itself.

The now-standard definition of displaced workers used by government and many private researchers was developed in conjunction with the DWS. In their report on the initial findings of the survey, analysts at the BLS defined displaced workers as those who, through no fault of their own, have lost jobs in which they have several years tenure and a considerable investment in skill development (Flaim and Sehgal 1985:2). To identify individuals who have lost a job through no fault of their own, they excluded the job loss due to seasonal employment, to self-owned business failures, and to "other," not easily classified reasons. The latter category presumably includes individuals dismissed for cause (i.e., fired) as well as some voluntary quits. They then classified as displaced the civilian, nonagricultural workers who reported losing a job due to a plant closure, slack work, or the abolishment of a shift or position.

Although the distinctions between layoffs, firings, and quits are not always clear from the reasons individuals give for a job loss, these restrictions are certainly defensible. They are consistent with the definition of displacement as an involuntary and permanent job loss resulting from employment shifts rather than inadequate job performance. Some analysts argue that permanent layoffs differ from plant closures in the sense that employers may have some discretion in determining who will be laid off and job performance is likely to influence that decision (Hamermesh 1989). However, it is the magnitude of the job loss due to slack work and the abolishment of shifts and positions that is of concern, and those employment shifts occur for reasons unrelated to individual job performance. It can also be objected that some respondents are overly pessimistic in reporting their job loss as permanent, although they are in a better position to make that judgment than any survey analyst. Without knowing the extent of the measurement error due to inaccurate self-reporting, we may regard the totals from these categories of job loss as upper limits on the number of displaced workers.

To identify workers with a considerable investment in skill development, the BLS researchers also restricted the definition of displaced worker to those losing jobs that they had held for three years or more. This tenure restriction is intended to focus attention upon experienced workers whose skills may not be transferable to other jobs and who are therefore likely to have reemployment problems. Intended or not, it also reduces the estimated size of the displaced work force by more than half. There are at least two different reasons for criticizing the use of job tenure to define displaced workers (see Moore 1990). First, it assumes that the length of time spent on a job accurately measures the time invested acquiring skills. However, many workers are trained in the course of holding several jobs with the same employer, and many skills are specific to an industry or occupation. Skill development is better measured, therefore, by years of experience within the industry or occupation from which many individuals are also displaced. Since this information is not available in the DWS, defining displaced workers in terms of the length of tenure in their previous job is simply a concession to the limitations of the survey data.

Second and more importantly, use of the tenure criterion implicitly equates the costs of displacement with the loss of specific skills. There is no question

Table 2.1.   Reasons for Job Displacement

	Survey period				
Reasons	1982–83	1984–85	1986–87	1988–89	1990–91
Plant closed	2,222	2,051	2,046	1,815	2,415
Slack work	2,922	2,094	1,790	1,441	2,984
Position/shift abolished	689	678	649	622	952
Total[a]	5,833	4,823	4,484	3,878	6,352

[a] Number in thousands of workers aged 20 to 64 displaced from the civilian, nonagricultural labor force.

that the earnings ability of workers is impaired when the training which they have acquired over several years is suddenly rendered superfluous. All else equal, the longer the time spent on the previous job, the greater the wage reduction when reemployed. But many short-tenure workers have difficulty finding new jobs and experience substantial wage losses when reemployed because the employment shifts that displace people also eliminate jobs and production processes. Large-scale job loss often results in a shift to lower-value production and to lower wage rates within local labor markets, regardless of the skills and experience of the individuals affected. Where opportunities for high-wage employment decline, the social costs of displacement are reflected less in the loss of specific skills than in the inability of those displaced to find jobs offering comparable wages.

For these reasons, the estimates of the size of the displaced population presented in Table 2.1 are based upon the now-standard definition of displaced worker without the tenure restriction. The figures in this table represent the weighted sample of civilian, nonagricultural workers between the ages of twenty and sixty-four who lost a job due to a plant closing, slack work, or the abolishment of a shift or position. To avoid any overlap in the coverage periods of the surveys, I include only those displaced during the two years preceding the date of each survey.[2] Thus the 1984 survey covers those displaced during 1982 and 1983, the 1986 survey those displaced during 1984 and 1985, and so forth. The figures in the table indicate that roughly two to three million people were displaced each year from 1982 to 1991. Breaking this total down by reason for job loss reveals a fairly consistent pattern. The number of jobs lost due to slack work changes over the business cycle, increasing markedly during the two recessionary periods. This does not mean that these recessionary layoffs were temporary. The rate of displacement increased during the downturns because the firms in many industries, most notably autos and steel, used recessionary layoffs to reduce permanently the size of their work force. The number of jobs lost due to plant closures and even to the abolishment of positions also fluctuates over the course of the business cycle, but much less so. The magnitude of the job loss throughout the decade shows the extent to which worker displacement has become a permanent feature of the American economy.

THE CHANGING INCIDENCE OF DISPLACEMENT

Some individuals run a greater risk of being displaced than others, largely because of employment shifts within the industry in which they work. Changes in the composition of the displaced work force mirror changes in the industry location of job loss, and there have been major industry-employment shifts over the past decade. These employment shifts can be seen in the number of jobs lost within various industries, but a better measure is the changing rate, or risk, of displacement for the typical worker. This displacement rate is the percentage of preretirement-age workers within an industry, occupation, or labor force group who lost a job for the reasons mentioned above.[3]

Table 2.2 shows the number of jobs lost and the associated risk of displacement within various industries and labor force groups during the two-year coverage period of each survey. While the number of jobs lost is self-explanatory, an example may help to clarify the meaning of displacement risk. During the 1982–83 period, 12.7 percent of manufacturing workers were displaced. Consequently, for the typical worker the relative probability or risk of being displaced at some point during those two years was 12.7 percent. Looking down the columns of Table 2.2, we can compare the number of jobs lost and the displacement risk within each industry or group. Comparing across the survey periods shows how the two measures changed over time.

The location of job loss shifted away from manufacturing and toward the service sector over the past decade. The number of workers displaced from manufacturing decreased steadily from over 2.5 million in 1982–83 to 1.2 million in 1988–89, before increasing to 1.8 million in 1991–92. Over the same period, the number of workers displaced from most service industries increased substantially. Comparing the two recessionary periods, the number of jobs lost increased by at least 30 percent in wholesale and retail trade and in nonprofessional services; it nearly doubled in professional services; and it more than tripled in finance, insurance, and real estate (FIRE). Service sector employment also grew during this period, but not as rapidly as job loss. As a result, the risk of displacement increased by more than three percentage points in FIRE and by a little less than a percentage point in professional services and in trade. In contrast, the displacement rate within manufacturing dropped by nearly four percentage points, from 12.7 to 8.8 percent. Despite these changes, the risk of job loss remains relatively high in

Table 2.2.   Number and Percentage of Workers Displaced during Each Survey Period, by Industry and Labor Force Group[a]

	Survey period				
	1982–83	1984–85	1986–87	1988–89	1990–91
Industry[b]					
Manufacturing	2,548	2,017	1,299	1,176	1,824
	(12.7)	(9.6)	(6.2)	(5.5)	(8.8)
TCU	393	366	266	214	357
	(5.8)	(4.9)	(3.4)	(2.6)	(4.4)
Trade	1,006	783	1,011	911	1,319
	(4.8)	(3.5)	(4.4)	(3.8)	(5.5)
FIRE	131	132	236	229	409
	(2.1)	(1.9)	(3.1)	(3.2)	(5.4)
Services					
Professional	312	296	394	345	597
	(1.5)	(1.4)	(1.7)	(1.4)	(2.3)
Nonprofessional	556	547	490	428	745
	(5.5)	(4.8)	(3.9)	(3.2)	(5.4)
Group					
Male	3,700	3,042	2,679	2,235	3,874
	(7.2)	(5.6)	(4.8)	(3.8)	(6.6)
Female	2,133	1,780	1,805	1,643	2,478
	(5.4)	(4.2)	(4.0)	(3.4)	(5.1)
White[c]	5,118	4,240	3,910	3,426	5,568
	(6.2)	(4.9)	(4.3)	(3.6)	(5.8)
Black	715	582	574	452	783
	(8.3)	(6.1)	(5.6)	(4.1)	(7.0)

[a] Number in thousands and percentage of civilian employees age 20 to 64 within each industry or labor force group who were displaced.
[b] Mining, construction, and public administration are not shown.
[c] Includes other races.

manufacturing which experienced an absolute decline in employment during the 1980s. The displacement rates within different industry sectors have converged; they are not equal.

Table 2.2 also shows the number and percentage of men and women, and of blacks and whites, displaced during each survey period. The industry location of job loss accounts for much of the change in the gender and race composition of the displaced population. Males and racial minorities are both overrepresented within the manufacturing work force, and both experience a relatively high rate of displacement. As the economy moved out of recession in the latter half of the decade and manufacturing employment stabilized, the risk of job loss became markedly more equal for different labor force groups. These gender and race differences widened again during the 1990–91 recession. But if we compare the two recessionary periods, the rates of job loss among men and women and among whites and blacks appear to have converged, just as they have between industry sectors.

Public anxiety over job loss may be a reaction to more than the number of workers involved. It may also reflect the changing educational background and occupational identity of those displaced. The perception that white-collar workers in general, and highly educated professional and managerial employees in particular, have become increasingly vulnerable to displacement is based upon more than personal observation. Academic works, as well as numerous articles in the popular and business press, have examined the growing threat that job loss poses to the economic security and middle-class status of highly educated workers.[4] In a passage reminiscent of the opening line of a well-known political manifesto, the author of a *Business Week* cover story dramatizes this threat:

> After years of layoffs, the specter of downward mobility is haunting legions of once-secure managers and professionals. They face permanent loss of the income, possessions, and status long considered the defining elements of middle-class life. (Nussbaum 1992:57)

The vulnerability of highly educated and skilled workers to labor market turbulence has both economic and social repercussions. Throughout this book it is argued that stable employment relationships contribute to economic growth, and this is particularly true for highly skilled workers. The assurance of long-term employment motivates individuals to acquire specific skills and training, and this skill development improves productivity. As the employment relationship becomes more tenuous, both firms and workers may be less willing to invest in training. Stable employment also contributes to productivity gains by facilitating the spread of new technologies. The ability and willingness of firms to adopt new technologies and to implement new work processes depends upon the flexibility and skills of their employees, and hence upon the stability of the employment relationship. Increased job insecurity thus represents a drag upon potential productivity growth.

The changing incidence of job loss also helps to explain the public uneasiness during the recent recession. Judged by the overall unemployment rate, the 1990–91 recession was comparatively mild. But if skilled, white-collar workers with long tenure are now at greater risk of displacement, their increased vulnerability would have heightened middle-class anxieties during the downturn. The status and influence of these individuals within the workplace and the community, and the fact that they have been relatively protected from displacement in the past, give added significance to their job loss. This may account for the widespread perception that the recent recession was qualitatively different from previous downturns.

The figures in Table 2.3 shed some light upon these concerns. They compare the number and percentage of workers displaced during the past two recessionary periods, 1982–83 and 1990–91, broken down by occupation, education, and age. As we might expect given the extent of job loss within manufacturing, during both of these periods blue-collar workers were at much greater risk of displacement than white-collar and service workers. The weight of job loss also fell more heavily upon younger, less-experienced workers and upon the less-educated.[5]

Although this general pattern characterizes both recessions, the incidence of displacement shifted somewhat from blue-collar to white-collar occupations, and from younger and less-educated to older and more-educated individuals. Half a million fewer blue-collar workers lost their jobs during the 1990–91 period than during 1982–83. For every other occupational category, the number of workers displaced was greater during the recent recession. The number displaced from managerial and administrative jobs showed a particularly large increase, rising from 477,000 to 723,000, or more than 50 percent. Much of this increase can be ascribed to the rapid growth of white-collar employment, but the rate of displacement also rose among white-collar and service workers, while falling by more than three percentage points among nonskilled blue-collars workers. The risk of job loss for different occupational groups has partly converged.

Table 2.3.   Number and Percentage of Workers Displaced, by Occupation, Education, and Age[a]

	Number displaced		Displacement rate	
	1982–83	1990–91	1982–83	1990–91
Occupation				
Manager	477	723	(4.4)	(4.9)
Professional	305	419	(2.4)	(2.6)
Technical, sales, and administrative support	1,376	1,787	(4.4)	(4.9)
Service	402	575	(2.9)	(3.6)
Skilled blue-collar	1,193	1,218	(9.9)	(9.1)
Other blue-collar	2,031	1,574	(12.4)	(9.0)
Education				
<12 years	1,313	1,045	(8.9)	(8.3)
12 years	2,698	2,495	(8.6)	(6.5)
>12 years	1,822	2,760	(5.4)	(5.8)
Age				
20–24	1,295	991	(9.4)	(8.0)
25–44	3,278	3,866	(6.6)	(6.0)
45–64	1,260	1,495	(4.6)	(4.8)

[a] Number in thousands and percentage of civilian employees age 20 to 64 within each occupation, age, or educational category who were displaced.

The weight of job loss also shifted toward older and more-educated workers during the recent recession. For those with a high school education or less, the probability of displacement was slightly lower in 1990–91 than in 1982–83. For those with at least some college, the probability of job loss was slightly higher during the recent recession. Similarly, the displacement rate was lower for younger workers but not for those between the ages of forty-five and sixty-four. The magnitude of these changes is modest, and there does not appear to be any increase in the probability of displacement among workers with lengthy job tenure (Farber 1993:20–21). Nonetheless, the changing industry and occupational location of job loss means that the employment relationships of college-educated workers are more vulnerable to disruption.

In summary, the pattern of labor market adjustment is changing. The goods-producing sector bore the brunt of the adjustment during the 1982–83 recession, and the weight of job loss fell disproportionately upon blue-collar workers. The impact of the recent recession was felt more evenly across industries and occupations. The number of workers displaced from white-collar and especially managerial jobs increased and so too did the risk of displacement. Growing numbers of older and better-educated workers were also displaced. These changes should not be overstated. White-collar jobs continue to be more stable than blue-collar employment, and older and college-educated workers are still less vulnerable to displacement than their younger and less-educated counterparts. Still, the differences are narrowing. There is little evidence of the employment stability that we expect with a more experienced and better-educated work force or with service-based, white-collar jobs. Instead, the risk of job loss has spread more evenly throughout the work force.

A DIGRESSION ON THE CAUSES OF EARNINGS LOSS

Displacement reduces average earnings because many individuals experience spells of unemployment, but the greater part of the earnings loss is due to lower reemployment wages. Most displaced workers received higher wages on their former jobs than they are able to earn elsewhere. There are several reasons why workers may receive a wage premium, or above-market wages, from an employer, and why they are likely to receive lower wages following displacement. Before we look at the economic costs of dislocation, a brief digression on the reasons for earnings loss is in order. These same reasons help to explain the earnings differences among workers who are not displaced and figure prominently in the analysis of earnings inequality presented in Chapter 5.

The first reason for the lower reemployment earnings of many displaced workers hinges upon the distinction between skills that enhance productivity across a wide range of work situations and skills that are specific to a workplace and of value only to a particular employer. This distinction is best explained within the context of human capital theory. The basic premise of human capital theory is that individuals undergo schooling and skills training in order to maximize the present value of their lifetime earnings. Training increases productivity and future earnings but it also entails costs, including the direct costs of schooling and the wages forgone during the training period. These costs represent an investment on which the individual expects to earn a return in the form of higher future earnings. For example, in deciding whether or not to attend college, individuals (or their parents) weigh both the costs and the benefits of that educational investment. The costs equal the earnings that the individual forgoes by attending college rather than entering the work force after high school, plus the tuition and related expenses. The benefits equal the present value of the additional lifetime earnings that one can expect with a college education. In economic terms, individuals become indifferent about attending college when the costs equal the benefits, that is, when the forgone earnings and tuition expenses equal the present value of the additional future earnings that they expect a college education will bring.

Human capital theory thus represents a very formal way of thinking about the individual investment aspect of education and training. No one knows exactly when the costs of additional schooling equal its financial rewards, and many people seek additional education even when the costs exceed those rewards. After all, schooling confers intrinsic as well as extrinsic benefits, and most people place some value upon education in and of itself. What is important in the present context is that individuals invest in skills that enhance their future earnings through on-the-job training, as well as through schooling, and these skills are both of a general nature and specific to the workplace (Becker 1975). Employers are hesitant to provide general skills training for fear that they will not be able to recoup their training investment. Purely general skills enhance individual productivity in any workplace and therefore have a market value. Employers who provide such training, and then attempt to recover their costs by paying the already-trained workers less than the market wage, are likely to lose both their employees and their investment. Therefore, individuals are likely to pay for general skills training, either by going to school or by accepting a lower wage than they could get elsewhere while they are being trained.

The situation is different with regard to skills that increase productivity only within a particular workplace. Because both employer and employee benefit from the acquisition of firm-specific skills, both will want to maintain the employment relationship. The best way to do that is for the employer to pay workers with valued skills more than they would receive elsewhere, but less than their value to the firm (i.e., their marginal revenue product). Workers who receive a wage premium are less likely to quit and are more likely to wait to be called back when they are laid off. And employers who pay skilled workers less than their value to the firm are less likely to lay them off in the first place for fear of losing them.[6]

When displacement does occur, it affects the earnings ability of workers by rendering these specific skills superfluous. It eliminates or devalues all of the resources that are specific to the abandoned activity, and those resources include firm-specific skills. In the case of individuals unable to find new employment in their former industry or occupation, they include skills that are specific to the industry or occupation as well. The efficient functioning of the economy requires the continuous learning of specific skills, and their sudden loss, or devaluation, imposes costs upon the larger society as well as the individuals directly affected. From this human capital perspective, it is efficient as well as equitable that these social costs of displacement be minimized and that they be widely shared.

The earnings losses of displaced workers cannot be attributed entirely to the elimination of specific skills. A second reason why some workers receive wage premiums is unionization. Their former job may have been covered by a collective bargaining agreement, in which case they benefited from the higher wages that union representation usually brings. Even if they were not covered, they may have worked within an industry where the threat of unionization had raised wages. In either case, the amount of the earnings loss following displacement will depend upon the size of the union wage premium and the likelihood of finding another job in a similarly unionized industry.

A related reason for why displaced workers often receive lower reemployment earnings has to do with the internal organization of the firm. The firms in many high-wage industries are characterized by internal labor markets, that is, by administrative rules and procedures that govern wage rates and the use of human resources. Firms with internal labor markets usually hire workers into entry-level jobs and then promote then along well-defined job ladders. Wages are tied to distinct job classifications on these ladders and movement up (or down) is governed largely by the length of employment. These hiring and promotion practices facilitate on-the-job training. They also maintain worker morale and effort by linking wages to tenure and by providing more senior employees with limited job security in the face of layoffs. Unfortunately, these benefits of internal labor markets are purchased at the cost of creating barriers to reemployment when workers are displaced (Osterman 1988). Since hiring is confined to entry-level positions, experienced workers are usually forced to start at the bottom and accept wage cuts. In addition, many employers hire entry-level workers for their flexibility rather than for acquired skills. They may believe that younger workers are more adaptable and more willing to accept an entry-level position. The prevalence of internal labor markets thus makes it difficult for displaced workers to find new jobs in their former industry or occupation.

Human capital theory is often criticized for disregarding the institutional aspects of the labor market that affect earnings. It would be more accurate to say that, within the context of human capital theory, only productivity-enhancing skills have social value. The earnings attributable to unionization, or to other institutional features of the labor market, are not thought to enhance productivity and are therefore viewed as "rents." Despite the hardships imposed upon individual workers and their families, the elimination of all unproductive rents is regarded as socially beneficial, and any earnings loss that results is purely private. It is not my purpose to assess the competing claims of human capital and institutional theories of earnings determination, but it is assumed here that the institutional features of the labor market enhance individual productivity as well as earnings. A final reason for the earnings losses of displaced workers explains how the "efficiency wages" associated with unionization and internal labor markets may contribute to productivity.

In conventional economic theory, the causal relationship between productivity and earnings runs one way. The wage rate is a function of marginal productivity; it equals the additional revenue generated by hiring an additional worker. In efficiency wage theory, the causal relationship runs both ways. Paying workers more than the market-clearing wage improves morale, reduces turnover and training costs, and encourages greater effort. Whenever these higher wages are then offset by increased productivity, it is efficient for firms to pay a wage premium. There are a number of variations on this theory, but they all share the basic assumption that paying above-market wages better enables employers to motivate, train, and retain workers and thereby improves productivity.[7]

As employment shifts away from industries in which unions, internal labor markets, and premium wages contribute to productivity, displacement results in earnings losses. Highly productive jobs and work processes are eliminated, and the earnings ability of individual workers is reduced as a result. That earnings loss is not purely private; it is part of the social cost of displacement. In other words, institutional changes in the labor market, as well as the elimination of specific skills, affect both productivity and earnings and thereby account for the lower reemployment wages of displaced workers.

THE EARNINGS LOSSES OF DISPLACED WORKERS

Turning from the reasons for earnings loss to the actual effect of displacement, this section examines the magnitude of the average wage reduction over time and across different labor force groups. As mentioned, the DWS was not designed to measure long-term earnings loss. Previous analyses of the survey show that a large fraction of those displaced experience wage reductions, but the limited time period over which earnings data are collected and the difficulty of constructing a comparison group of equivalent nondisplaced workers create a number of measurement problems. Estimates of the average long-term earnings loss based upon the DWS vary considerably (cf. Podgursky and Swaim 1987a; Kletzer 1989; Farber 1993).

In a recent study of the costs of worker displacement, Louis Jacobson, Robert LaLonde, and Daniel Sullivan (1993) addressed these problems by constructing a longitudinal data set from the administrative records of the State of Pennsylvania. By merging the quarterly earnings histories of workers with employment information on their firms, these researchers were able to estimate the impact of displacement upon lifetime earnings. A major limitation of this state administrative data is that it does not indicate whether the separation of worker and firm was the result of a layoff, a discharge for cause, or a voluntary quit. Since quits and discharges decrease sharply as job tenure increases, these researchers confined their sample to workers with six or more years of tenure. They further limited the sample to workers separating from firms undergoing employment declines of 30 percent or more so as to ensure that the dismissals were the result of economic restructuring. Looking at the size and temporal pattern of the earnings losses of these high-tenure workers between 1980 and 1986, they estimated the effect of displacement upon lifetime earnings.

The major findings of their study can be briefly summarized. First, the magnitude of the earnings loss of experienced workers is far greater than previous studies have shown. The earnings of displaced workers begin to diverge from their expected levels about three years prior to separation as firms resort to wage cuts, reduced overtime, and temporary layoffs in an effort to avoid closure or permanent cutbacks. In other words, earnings losses typically begin before workers separate from the firm, so comparing pre- and postdisplacement earnings, as is usually done, underestimates the total earnings reduction. The average discounted value of the earnings losses of these high-tenure workers from three years before to six years after separation amounted to $50,000. Projected to retirement, their average lifetime losses rose to $80,000. This total earnings loss includes the wage reductions prior to separation and the losses due to unemployment, but the greatest portion (about 72 percent) is the result of permanently lower reemployment earnings (Jacobson et al. 1993:137–44).

Second, the amount of the earnings reduction experienced by these high-tenure workers, especially for those displaced from manufacturing, varies depending upon whether or not they find new jobs in the same industry sector. The losses of manufacturing workers who found new jobs in the same industry were about half as large as the losses of those forced to take nonmanufacturing jobs. Finally, even when workers found jobs in the same four-digit industry, their wages averaged about 20 percent below the predisplacement level. The generality and pervasiveness of this reduction across different groups of workers led the authors to conclude that it is not explained by the union wage premiums or efficiency wages prevalent within particular industries. When high-tenure workers are displaced, some firm-specific determinant of earnings is lost.

On the basis of these findings, the authors argue that existing employment and training programs do not and cannot adequately compensate the victims of economic restructuring. Income replacement programs offset only a very small portion of the average earnings loss of these displaced workers. Unemployment insurance (UI) replaces part of the income loss in the year following separation, but it has no effect upon living standards over the long-term. Most of the earnings reduction is due to lower future wages, and the only way to redress that is to increase the reemployment wage. Job search assistance is of greatest value when it helps workers find jobs in their former industry and occupation, but most programs try to move individuals into available jobs as quickly as possible with little regard to their long-term earnings. Even when job search assistance enables workers to find new jobs in the same industry, it will not eliminate the 20 percent drop in earnings that typically results from displacement. Nor do public training programs adequately compensate for the loss of firm-specific skills. As we shall see, most classroom training programs are too limited in duration to have much effect upon reemployment earnings.

According to these analysts, the most efficient way to compensate displaced workers is through a wage subsidy program. They estimate that a subsidy for reemployed, high-tenure workers that replaced four-sevenths of each dollar of lost wages over their working lives would cost about $9 billion a year, while a subsidy that lasted only two years beyond their UI claims would cost about $2 billion (Jacobson et al. 1993:167–68). Compensating reemployed workers for part of their wage loss would lessen resistance to environmental and trade policies that benefit the larger society, while at the same time preserving workers' incentive to find new employment and to seek higher earnings. Unfortunately, the budgetary impact of this policy makes its enactment very unlikely, and it does not give employers any incentive to avoid layoffs or dismissals. Wage subsidies also fail to address the larger problem of how to minimize the loss of earnings ability when workers are forced to find new jobs.

The Jacobson, LaLonde, and Sullivan study presents the best estimates to date of the lifetime earnings losses of displaced workers. Those losses are much larger than previously thought, and they are mostly due to lower reemployment wages. The lack of demographic information in state administrative data prevented these researchers from looking at how earnings losses vary with educational level and occupation. The DWS was not designed to measure long-term earnings reductions, but it does include demographic information and asks respondents about both their current and former weekly earnings. It thus enables us to compare the relative wage loss of different groups of displaced workers over the ten-year coverage period of the surveys.

The percentages in the top line of Table 2.4 represent the proportionate wage loss of all displaced workers, as calculated from the DWS.[8] Those relative wage losses (which surely are underestimates) amounted to about 13 percent of the predisplacement wage during the 1980s and rose to more than 17 percent in the recent recession. The figures below the top line compare the average wage reductions among men and women, and among whites and blacks, and find little difference. Although there is no consistent difference in the proportionate wage loss of race and gender groups, it should be kept in mind that the predisplacement earnings of women and racial minorities are typically much less than those of males and whites. Female and minority workers are also more likely to experience prolonged jobless spells following a job loss, something that is discussed in the following chapter.

There are substantial differences in the percentage wage reduction among occupational groups, and these relative losses have shifted over

Table 2.4. Percentage Real Wage Loss (Gain) of Reemployed Workers

	Survey period				
	1982–83	*1984–85*	*1986–87*	*1988–89*	*1990–91*
All workers[a]	13.1	14.0	12.9	10.9	17.5
Male	15.5	12.3	13.4	9.8	19.0
Female	8.2	16.7	12.0	12.5	15.3
White	13.2	14.0	12.6	10.5	17.4
Black	11.9	13.9	14.9	14.9	18.8
Occupation					
Manager	11.5	13.6	15.3	20.9	23.7
Professional	1.0	1.7	7.8	(2.0)	8.4
Technical, sales, and administrative support	6.7	10.0	7.9	7.6	11.4
Service	12.2	15.5	0.2	(3.3)	15.6
Skilled blue-collar	16.3	19.4	15.9	9.8	23.1
Other blue-collar	19.3	15.8	21.1	18.2	20.7
Education					
<12 years	25.5	22.5	25.2	10.9	19.7
12 years	12.1	16.7	11.9	12.8	15.6
>12 years	7.9	6.3	8.1	8.7	18.4
Age					
20–24	6.4	3.4	1.3	2.9	12.8
25–44	10.5	13.9	11.9	10.2	17.1
45–64	30.8	25.8	25.9	19.9	22.5

[a] Workers reemployed as of the date of the survey.

time. Displaced blue-collar workers, both skilled and nonskilled, sustained wage reductions of approximately 15 to 20 percent throughout this ten-year period. In contrast, the proportionate earnings losses among white-collar groups were initially smaller but increased substantially in the 1992 survey. Again, the most notable change occurred among managerial employees. The percentage wage loss among managers and administrators rose continuously over the decade, increasing from 11.5 percent in the 1984 survey to nearly 24 percent in the 1992 survey. The wage losses of professional employees and of technical, sales, and administrative support personnel also increased, but not continuously or by so much.

The wage reductions of workers displaced during the recent recession were particularly large, and there is some evidence that the costs of job loss shifted toward highly educated, white-collar workers. In addition to the difficulties of managers and administrators, the proportionate wage losses of those with at least some college education jumped from roughly 8 percent in the 1980s to over 18 percent at the beginning of this decade. Better-educated workers usually incur smaller losses following displacement, but this was not the case during the 1990–91 period. The unusually large earnings reductions during the recent recession were spread more evenly across occupational and demographic groups. As was the case with the changing risks of displacement, the overall pattern is one of convergence.

DISPLACEMENT AND DOWNWARD MOBILITY

Widespread job loss has become a salient feature of our national economic life. The magnitude of employment loss fluctuates over the business cycle, but between 1982 and 1991 an average of more than two million civilian, nonagricultural workers were displaced each year. Most of this job loss was permanent. It was the result of structural changes in the economy and should not be equated with cyclical unemployment.

The typical job loser is still a blue-collar, industrial worker, but this modal type is becoming less representative as employment shifts to the service sector. The proportion of the work force employed in service industries increased by six percentage points during the 1980s, and three-fourths of all jobs are located today within this sector (Plunkert 1990). The service sector employs a growing proportion of the work force, and it accounts for a growing share of job loss. In addition, the composition of the displaced population depends upon the rate of displacement within different industries and occupations. Over the ten-year period covered by the surveys, the rate of job loss decreased in manufacturing while increasing in FIRE, in professional services, and in wholesale and retail trade—industries that employ a disproportionate number of workers in white-collar occupations. Because of both the shift of employment to the service sector and the growing rate of job loss within that sector, the workers displaced toward the end of the past decade represented a wider range of industries and occupations than those displaced at the beginning. Although the risks of job loss have converged across occupations and demographic groups, they are not equal. The displacement rate is much higher among blue-collar than white-collar workers, and younger and less-educated individuals are still at greater risk of losing a job than their older and better-educated counterparts.

Displacement and dislocation are not synonymous. Many displaced workers quickly find new jobs paying comparable wages, while others endure lengthy jobless spells only to sustain large wage reductions when they are reemployed. The latter are dislocated as well as displaced, and they bear most of the costs of labor market adjustment. The lifetime earnings losses of long-tenure workers are substantial, especially for those displaced from manufacturing industries and blue-collar occupations. Since employment is shifting to white-collar occupations, the number of white-collar jobs being created more than offsets the number lost. Displaced white-collar workers therefore have a relatively good chance of finding new jobs within their former occupation, while those displaced from industrial, blue-collar jobs often lose the skills that define their working lives. Even during the recent recession when the costs as well as the risks of displacement were more equally shared across occupational groups, white-collar workers were much more likely to find a new job within their former occupation.[9] Because of these industry and occupational growth trends, blue-collar workers bore the brunt of the recent downturn, just as they have of previous recessions.

Nonetheless, increasing numbers of white-collar workers are experiencing economic dislocation. Comparing the average reemployment wage of those displaced during the past two recessions reveals a sharp earnings decline among college-educated and white-collar workers. The percentage wage reduction of those who lost managerial jobs increased steadily throughout the 1980s. Faced with an intensifying domestic and foreign competition and with the growing threat of takeover, firms throughout the economy have restructured and downsized, making highly educated, white-collar workers more vulnerable to job loss. Corporate downsizing has also altered traditional career patterns by reducing opportunities for upward mobility. The earnings profiles of millions of white-collar and managerial employees have flattened. The implicit contract that guaranteed the employment security of managerial and professional employees is being rewritten, and the terms of the new contract have heightened career anxieties. Surveys show a prolonged decline in the confidence with which managers view their careers, and this declining confidence is linked to corporate restructuring (Doeringer et al. 1991:163–64). The recent recession simply gave a focus to anxieties that have been building for over a decade.

The labor market turbulence of the past decade has affected occupational groups that long felt relatively secure in their jobs, and their anxiety over economic dislocation and the threat of downward mobility has profound social and political implications. It is reflected in the volatility of the electorate and in the quiet and not so quiet desperation that characterizes millions of work lives. The perceived loss of employment security also affects attitudes toward inequality and distributional issues. People who are preoccupied with the threat to their jobs and earnings become indifferent to the hardships of those at the bottom of an ever more divided society. Perhaps the greatest danger to the loss of employment security among highly educated, white-collar workers is that it blinds them, and us, to the far bleaker economic prospects of those who are less skilled and less advantaged.

NOTES

1. This point is emphasized by Seitchik (1991:52–53).

2. This procedure also minimizes recall bias, the tendency of respondents to fail to recall past job losses. Because of the retrospective nature of the data, the DWS underestimates the extent of the job loss that occurred several years prior to the interview dates.

3. Displacement rates were calculated as the ratio of the number of displaced workers within a labor force category over a given two-year period to the average number of preretirement-age employees within that category as reported in *Employment and Earnings*, various years.

4. For an anthropological account of the downward mobility of many middle-class Americans, see Newman (1988). The discussion of the mobility consequences of displacement presented here draws upon the econometric analysis in Farber (1993).

5. These associations are not spurious. The risk of displacement is inversely and independently related to education, age, and the length of job tenure (see Farber 1993:12–13).

6. Employers are also under less pressure to lay off workers with firm-specific skills during business downturns since they are paid less than their marginal revenue product.

7. For a review of efficiency wage theories see Thaler (1989).

8. The proportionate earnings losses in Table 2.4 were calculated by subtracting the log of the real weekly earnings on the former job from the log of the real weekly wage at the date of the survey. Exponentiating the average of this log difference yields the proportionate earnings reductions in the table. Former earnings were deflated using the 1982–84 = 100 consumer price index for the year of displacement, and current earnings were deflated using the January CPI for the survey year.

9. The number of blue-collar jobs reported in *Employment and Earnings* fell by 2.4 million (a 7.3 percent decline) while the number of managerial jobs increased by 185,000 (a 1.2 percent gain) between July 1990, when the recession began, and December 1991.

Long-Term Joblessness and Labor Market Disadvantage 3

Plant closings exemplify the labor market disruption caused by mass layoffs. Excluding those who took early retirement, more than half of the former Chrysler workers at the Kenosha assembly plant were out of work for over a year. The stories of plant closings are sometimes criticized for presenting worst-case scenarios, but the unemployment experience of the Chrysler workers is not that unusual. Labor force surveys such as the DWS show that a large percentage of displaced workers remain jobless for long periods. The work lives of a sizable fraction of the displaced population are severely disrupted, and the difficulties they experience finding new jobs are indicative of labor market disadvantage. For these individuals, earnings losses do not represent the full costs of displacement.[1] The loss of the work role also entails adverse social and psychological consequences. All too often, the full costs of displacement include the detrimental effects of prolonged joblessness.

Conventional explanations of unemployment duration give little weight to the social and psychological benefits of the work role. They portray unemployment as an investment in job search and attribute the length of unemployment spells primarily to wage expectations. The basic premise of all search theories is that the information needed to make optimal decisions is difficult and costly to obtain.[2] To be sure of making the best possible choice, whether with regard to a job, a marriage partner, or anything else, an individual would have to sample all of the available offers. In the case of job search, a more cost-effective strategy is to decide beforehand upon a minimally acceptable, or reservation, wage and accept the first job offer that meets that standard. The decision to accept employment—and the length of the preceding unemployment spell—thus hinges upon what the job-seeker considers to be an acceptable wage offer. The higher the reservation wage, the smaller the proportion of available jobs that will be judged acceptable, and the longer the expected period of search to find one that is acceptable.

Just as individuals increase their earnings ability by acquiring marketable skills, they increase the return on those skills by seeking out the best-possible job match. As long as job search results in better matches between the preferences and skills of individual workers and the requirements and rewards of jobs, unemployment spells are economically productive. More precisely, search unemployment is productive as long as the expected benefit from finding a better job exceeds any available wage offer. When the costs of search—and especially the wages forgone while unemployed—exceed this expected benefit, wage expectations should adjust. They should fall into line with available employment opportunities.

The reservation wage thus balances the cost of search against the benefit of making a better job match. Anything that raises or lowers the costs of job search also affects the reservation wage and the average duration of unemployment spells. Conservative analysts emphasize this aspect of job search theory in attributing higher unemployment to increased social welfare spending. Income supports such as unemployment compensation replace part of the earnings loss that people incur while unemployed. The availability of unemployment benefits reduces the cost of continued job search and thereby raises the reservation wage. Job-seekers are more likely to turn down unattractive offers, to engage in longer periods of search, and to make better eventual job matches. Of course, the longer the average unemployment spell, the greater the number of people unemployed at any given time. The actual effect of income supports upon contemporary unemployment is discussed more fully in Chapter 6, but it is important to point out that good job matches benefit society as well as individual job-seekers. Stable employment relationships and economic growth depend upon workers finding jobs to which they are committed and through which they can acquire experience and skills, and unemployment compensation increases the chances of making a good job match.

Viewed in terms of the investment logic of job search theory, unemployment is the result of choices made within the constraints of imperfect information. The reservation wage occupies a central place in this theory because it defines the decision rule for accepting or rejecting job offers, and the emphasis upon wage expectations and individual choice portrays most unemployment as voluntary. Needless to say, the experience of millions of displaced workers is hard to reconcile with the voluntarism of search theory. To be effective, job search depends upon the availability of jobs and of information about those jobs. Tight labor markets can easily discourage active search or render it futile, and access to labor market information is gained through social networks. Yet once we acknowledge that the duration of unemployment spells depends upon the efficiency of job search, and not just upon individual wage expectations, search theory provides a useful framework for analyzing the duration of unemployment. Stripped of the voluntarist emphasis upon individual choice, it helps us to identify the sources of labor market disadvantage.

By definition, displaced workers are involuntary job losers. Whether or not we characterize the length of their jobless spells as voluntary, many encounter a number of obstacles that limit the effectiveness of job search. Like the former Chrysler workers, they may find that the demand for their experience and skills has collapsed, and they face a number of difficulties in acquiring new skills or in searching beyond the local labor market. The lack of educational background or credentials can impede job search by limiting access to formal sources of information. Without educational qualifications, job-seekers rely primarily upon personal contacts and social networks for job leads, and their search is correspondingly restricted. Discriminatory hiring practices also constrain job search. Older, more experienced workers often encounter age discrimination and confront hiring and promotion practices that favor younger workers. Women and racial minorities frequently face overt discrimination, and the latter are disadvantaged by a residential segregation and isolation that limits access to both information and jobs.

Where the constraints upon effective job search overlap, they represent a formidable barrier to reemployment. Many displaced workers are unable to find jobs that pay wages comparable to what they have received, or to what similarly qualified workers still receive. Forced to engage in a lengthy and unproductive search, they enter a period of transitional unemployment that leads either to labor force withdrawal or to a drastic lowering of expectations. Eventually, the length of the jobless spell itself becomes an obstacle to reemployment. Prolonged unemployment involves psychological as well as material deprivation, and its adverse effects impact upon job search and compound the problems of many job-seekers.

The rest of this chapter explains more fully why some displaced workers are more likely than others to remain jobless for long periods. It discusses the reemployment problems of less-educated and older workers, as well as those of racial minorities, and presents information from the DWS on the extent of their long-term joblessness. It also discusses the social psychological importance of the work role and the negative effects of prolonged unemployment. These detrimental effects are also part of the cost of displacement.

THE LABOR MARKET DISADVANTAGE
OF LESS-EDUCATED AND OLDER WORKERS

We have already seen how investments in education and in specific job skills help to account for the earnings losses of displaced workers. Those same investments affect the length of unemployment spells. Increased education is associated with shorter periods of unemployment both because it provides general skills that are of value to employers and because it improves the efficiency of job search. It is the latter reason that is of primary interest here. To find a job, one needs to know, or at least suspect, where new employment opportunities exist, and highly educated individuals enjoy a number of advantages in locating suitable jobs.

Descriptive accounts of the job search process often distinguish between formal and informal sources of labor market information (e.g., Kelvin and Jarrett 1985:27–41). Formal sources of information include advertised openings as well as public and private employment agencies. Education provides access to these sources of information and better enables individuals to utilize that information. Educational credentials introduce and recommend the jobseeker to prospective employers. They define the occupational identity of the applicant and the type of job being sought, and thereby limit the area of search. By matching applicants to interested employers and suitable jobs, educational qualifications enable job-seekers to use formal sources of information more effectively.

In contrast, those without certified training or skills often engage in a tiring and unstructured search. Lacking access to formal sources of information, they are necessarily dependent upon informal networks of family and friends. Informal sources of information are useful to all job-seekers, but they are crucial to the success of those who depend upon personal contacts for job leads. Most networks are local and take time to establish, and being dependent upon them restricts the area of job search. Individuals with limited education or training also rely upon family and friends for personal recommendation. For them, relocating means losing the personal contacts and recommendations that are crucial to successful search. Because this dependence upon informal networks and personal contacts restricts their mobility, the less educated are vulnerable to local employment shifts. Once displaced, they are likely to be dislocated as well.

Unlike education, age and work experience are directly associated with longer unemployment spells. Many older and more senior workers have spent years acquiring job-specific skills that are rendered superfluous by displacement. They face the prospect of large wage reductions upon reemployment, so it is not surprising that they tend to remain out of work for longer periods following a job loss. Apart from the loss of specific skills, age and experience are associated with longer unemployment because they constrain job search. Many older workers have strong attachments to community and friends, and their mobility is restricted by financial and emotional ties. Older workers are also disadvantaged by the effects of statistical discrimination. As a group, they have higher health care costs, and these costs are an important consideration in the hiring decisions of employers because health insurance in this country is usually purchased through the workplace.

The job search of many older workers is also rendered less effective by the institutional features of the labor market. In particular, the hiring and promotion practices that define internal labor markets often create barriers to the reemployment of older, more experienced workers. Internal labor markets provide on-the-job training and foster stronger attachment to the firm, but these benefits are achieved by limiting most hiring to entry-level jobs. Employers are therefore concerned about the wage expectations and adaptability of new hires. They may view the experience of older workers as a sign of high expectations and inflexibility. Internal labor markets are prevalent in manufacturing industries, and older workers displaced from these industries often find that employers are particularly hesitant to hire them. In their study of the decline of South Chicago's steel industry, David Bensman and Roberta Lynch quote a former mill foreman:

> I tell employers I'll take any job, even at $6 or $7 an hour, but they don't believe you. They see you worked at Wisconsin Steel and you can't get nothing. (1988:108)

Finally, the job search of older workers may be less effective because of cultural biases that have no economic rationale. It is little more than a truism to say that our society places too little value upon the maturity and breadth of experience that older workers bring to the workplace. This cultural bias persists even though studies consistently find that older workers are more reliable than younger ones, have better work attitudes, cost less to train, are absent less often, and are less likely to quit (Labich 1993). Yet despite the evidence of their value as employees, older workers continue to swell the ranks of those too discouraged to actively search for a job.

The reemployment difficulties of less-educated and older workers are evident in the DWS. The information in that survey enables us to examine the relationship between the personal characteristics of displaced workers and the duration of their jobless spells. For those who experience long periods without work, the distinction between being unemployed and being out of the work force ceases to be meaningful. The long-term jobless respond to changing labor market conditions by abandoning or by resuming active search; that is to say, they move out of or back into the work force. To measure the reemployment difficulties of displaced workers and not just whether they are currently unemployed, the DWS asks respondents how long they were without and available for work following displacement. In the 1988 and subsequent surveys the original wording of this question was altered to ensure that the reported jobless spell was continuous, with no intermittent period of employment.[3] This change of wording means that the different survey estimates of the average spell length are not strictly comparable. The reduced length of the average spell in the later surveys reflects the change in question wording as well as an improving business climate. For-

Table 3.1. Percentage of Displaced Workers Whose Jobless Spells Exceeded Six Months, by Worker Characteristics

	Survey years				
	1981–82	*1983–84*	*1985–86*	*1987–88*	*1989–90*
All workers[a]	49.1	35.9	29.8	33.2	32.1
Education					
<12 years	64.2	48.1	39.7	44.2	47.2
12 years	50.2	37.7	31.4	34.7	33.9
>12 years	37.9	26.6	23.0	26.0	25.0
Age					
20–24	41.2	27.9	19.5	26.6	22.0
25–44	48.7	33.6	27.6	31.8	28.7
45–64	59.1	49.2	43.7	41.4	46.4
Males	47.6	32.1	26.3	31.5	30.4
Females	51.8	41.9	35.1	35.5	34.4
White	46.7	33.1	28.5	32.1	31.2
Black	67.2	58.7	39.6	41.9	38.5

[a] Those aged 20 to 64 when displaced at least a year prior to the date of survey.

tunately, the change in wording does not obscure the group differences in long-term joblessness within each survey period.

Table 3.1 shows the percentage of displaced workers who were out of work for more than twenty-six weeks, broken down by education, age, gender, and race. To ensure that any jobless spells still in progress would have exceeded the twenty-six-week cutoff, each survey sample includes the respondents who were displaced over a two-year period but at least a year prior to the date of the survey. Thus the 1984 survey includes those displaced in 1981 and 1982, the 1986 survey covers the 1983–84 period, and so forth. The figures in the top line of the table show the overall percentage of long-term jobless in each survey. Judging from those figures, throughout the decade over 30 percent of those displaced remained out of work for more than six months.

The percentage of long-term jobless within each educational category follows a consistent and expected pattern. Displaced workers with less than a high school education are much more likely than their better-educated counterparts to endure long jobless spells. The specific figures vary, but in every survey period roughly 40 percent or more of those with less than a high school education reported jobless spells of over six months. This percentage declines sharply for high school graduates and those with at least some college. The percentage of long-term jobless among the different age groups also follows the expected pattern. The average spell length increases with age, and older workers between the ages of forty-five and sixty-four are much more likely to be represented among the long-term jobless. During each survey period, more than 40 percent of the displaced workers in this age group were out of work for more than six months.

THE LABOR MARKET DISADVANTAGE OF RACIAL MINORITIES

The figures in Table 3.1 also reveal large racial and gender differences in the duration of jobless spells. Displaced female and minority workers are overrepresented among the long-term jobless. These gender and racial disparities are not necessarily the result of overt discrimination, but they are indicative of labor market disadvantage. In the case of displaced female workers, the constraints of traditional family roles appear to account for much of the difference. Women are much more likely than men to cease active search and to withdraw from the labor force following a job loss. In contrast, the racial disparity is not explained by early labor force withdrawal. The labor force attachment of the two racial groups is closely comparable, yet there is a twenty-point difference in the percentages of black and white workers who remained jobless for more than six months in the 1984 and 1986 DWS, while the later surveys show approximately a ten-point gap.[4] This difference is due almost entirely to higher black unemployment (see Moore 1992).

The labor market disadvantage of racial minorities is often attributed to individual differences in education and work experience, but a more compelling explanation for the long-term joblessness of these minority workers emphasizes the conditions under which job search is conducted. For displaced workers in general, the effectiveness of job search depends upon the labor market demand for their skills. For racial minorities, the effectiveness of search also depends upon the social and residential barriers that limit access to both information and jobs. These obstacles to reemployment begin with the concentration and residential segregation of the black population. More than half of the black respondents in the DWS, compared to less than 20 percent of the whites, live within the central cities of major urban areas. This residential concentration closely approximates that of the black population as a whole and is most pronounced in the older, and more slowly growing cities of the Northeast and Midwest that are losing their traditional industrial base. Compared to whites, and even to Hispanic and Asian minorities, blacks remain concentrated and segregated within the central city and its adjacent suburbs (Massey and Denton 1993).

Employment patterns mirror these residential patterns. The farther one moves out from the central city, the smaller the proportion of the work force that is black (Leonard 1987). In part, the association between residence and employment is explained by the fact that distance limits the physical accessibility of jobs and the social accessibility of local labor market information. Distance increases the costs of looking for and commuting to work, and it removes job-seekers from the informal networks through which many jobs are found.[5] In larger part, the relationship between residential and employment patterns is explained by race rather than by space. The racial tensions and discrimination that limit residential choice also constrain the job search of many minority workers. Whether or not employers intentionally discriminate, they are very aware of the racial makeup and attitudes of the work force and community in which they are located. As the distance of an establishment from the central city increases, so does the likelihood that hiring practices will work to the advantage of a predominantly white work force.

Either because of the costs imposed by physical distance or because of racial tensions and discrimination, the employment search of many displaced black workers is confined to a smaller and more geographically concentrated set of jobs within urban areas. With the area of job search restricted, they face a more intense competition for the few attractive jobs that are accessible. This competition became all the more intense in recent years as many urban centers lost their traditional industrial base. Manufacturing has long been a major source of employment for racial minorities, and the loss of manufacturing industries and blue-collar jobs has contributed to their reemployment problems. Blacks displaced from manufacturing have been much less successful than whites at finding new jobs within their former industry (Kletzer 1991). As manufacturing shifts away from major urban centers, it is leaving the minority work force behind. And as we have seen, displaced workers who cannot find new jobs in the same industry usually suffer a large earnings loss.

This explanation for the lengthy jobless spells of many minority workers differs from the conventional emphasis upon wage expectations and individual choice by focusing instead upon the labor market obstacles to effective job search. The difference of interpretation may not appear to be very consequential, but it raises an important question. Are the reemployment difficulties of these displaced workers explained by wage demands that are relatively high or relatively slow to adjust to a decline in earnings ability? If so, this finding would be consistent with the conservative claim that social welfare spending has increased unemployment by reducing the costs of job search. The average predisplacement wage of blacks (and women) is less than that of whites (and men), and unemployment insurance and other income supports replace a larger portion of the earnings of lower-wage workers. The availability of income supports can be expected, therefore, to have a greater impact upon the reservation wage of displaced minority and female workers. Their relatively high wage expectations would then account for the longer jobless spells.

Labor force surveys do not directly measure wage expectations, but the DWS does include information on the weekly wage. To gauge the reservation wage of reemployed workers, we need only compare their current and former real weekly earnings. The reservation wage can be defined as the percentage of their former earnings that workers receive when they accept a new job. Since wage demands can be expected to adjust downward over time, we need to control for the length of the jobless spell. By comparing the percentage difference between the former and current wages of workers who were jobless for varying periods, we can see how the reservation wage changes. If the wage expectations of a particular group are relatively high or slow to adjust, those reemployed at any given point in time should incur smaller percentage wage losses. In other words, if the lengthy jobless spells of many minority workers are due to high wage expectations, we expect their reemployment wage to be relatively high. Or what amounts to the same thing, we expect their proportionate earnings losses to be comparatively small.

The figures in Table 3.2 are based upon the combined sample of reemployed workers from all five surveys. They measure the percentage real wage loss among different race and gender groups as the length of their jobless spells increases from less than fifteen weeks, to between fifteen and twenty-six weeks, to more than twenty-six weeks.[6] The wage losses of all reemployed workers, shown in the first column, increase from 5.0 percent of their former wage for those who found a new job within fourteen weeks, to 15.6 percent for those reemployed fifteen to twenty-six weeks after displacement, to 28.8 percent for those who were out of work for more than twenty-six weeks. The magnitude of these average wage losses over time is hard to reconcile with the voluntarism of job search theory. The increasing size of the percentage wage reduction indicates that prolonged job search does not result in better wage offers and is not productive. It seems unlikely, therefore, that many displaced workers are betting the forgone wages from an available job against the possibility of receiving a better wage offer sometime in the future.

Table 3.2. Percentage Wage Loss of Reemployed Workers, by Duration of Jobless Spell (Combined Samples)

Weeks jobless	All workers[a]	White males	Black males	White females	Black females
<15	5.0	5.8	8.0	2.3	11.8
15–26	15.6	17.9	14.5	12.6	12.5
>26	28.6	27.3	23.8	31.4	32.2

[a] Combined sample of reemployed workers, aged 20 to 64 when displaced during the two years prior to each survey date.

Table 3.2 also compares the wage losses of each race and gender group. The proportionate wage reduction among reemployed black workers increases sharply with the duration of their jobless spells and is comparable in magnitude to that of reemployed whites. The average loss among black males who remained out of work for more than six months amounted to nearly 24 percent of their former earnings, while the average loss of white males after a similar jobless spell was a little over 27 percent. The percentage wage losses of reemployed female workers were at least comparable to those of males. Black and white females who were jobless for more than six months accepted wage reductions of 32 and 31 percent, respectively. Even though the real predisplacement earnings of these minority and female workers are much lower than the earnings of their white and male counterparts, there is no evidence that their reservation wage is relatively slow to adjust downward. Given the magnitude and similarity of these losses, it is difficult to see how the wage demands of displaced female and minority workers could explain the group differences in long-term joblessness.

Individuals differ not only in their wage demands, but also in the abilities and effort that they bring to the search for employment. It is possible that the reemployment problems of many minority workers are simply the result of individual differences that affect job search. These differences are hard to observe directly, but they are reflected in and measurable through the educational background and previous employment history of experienced workers. More sophisticated analyses of the DWS therefore control statistically for a wide range of individual and family characteristics, including education and prior work experience. The results of these analyses indicate that the reemployment chances of displaced black workers are significantly less than those of whites, and this disparity is not explained by the personal characteristics or work experience that are generally thought to influence search behavior and the hiring decisions of employers.[7] The fact that these personal characteristics do not account for the racial disparity in joblessness is evidence of group disadvantage. Displaced black workers have to overcome greater obstacles in their job search and, as a result, experience greater difficulty than whites in finding another job.

THE SOCIAL-PSYCHOLOGICAL EFFECTS
OF PROLONGED UNEMPLOYMENT

Attributing the duration of unemployment spells to wage expectations alone not only ignores the institutional barriers to job search, it also overlooks the importance of the work role and the social and psychological effects of long-term joblessness. The meaning of the work role differs for white-collar and blue-collar workers, but its importance to individual well-being has long been documented by attitudinal surveys. White-collar workers are more likely to report that their jobs are interesting and provide a sense of accomplishment, while blue-collar workers place greater value upon the social interaction of the workplace and the way that the work role structures and occupies their time. But people in both occupational groups view unemployment and enforced idleness as a threat to their sense of self-worth, and most report that they would continue to work even if they had enough money to live comfortably (Morse and Weiss 1955).

The importance of the work role to individual and communal well-being emerges more starkly in ethnographic studies of the unemployed. In *Marienthal*, one of the first systematic, observational studies of mass unemployment, Marie Jahoda, Paul Lazarsfeld, and Hans Zeisel (1971) described the daily life of an unemployed Austrian community during the depths of the depression. First published in 1933, this sociological classic introduced many of the themes found in current studies of long-term unemployment. Perhaps the central theme, and one that recurs in nearly every ethnographic study of the unemployed, is the place of the work role in the temporal organization of daily life.[8] People organize their lives around the distinction between work and leisure. Leisure time is not defined by the absence of work: it is defined in relation to work. The loss of the work role is disorienting precisely because it disrupts this habitual time structure. Without the distinction between work and leisure, the residents of Marienthal had trouble using time effectively, or even keeping track of it. Domestic routines helped to maintain the temporal organization of daily life for the women, but most of the men drifted into an undifferentiated experience of time. In a telling example, the authors note that eighty-eight out of one hundred men surveyed did not wear a watch. Time and keeping time had lost their meaning.

In addition to structuring time, work gives a sense of purpose and meaning to nonwork life activity. The workplace is a source of contacts and personal networks, and the work role becomes an important basis of social interaction. Individuals who are cut off from the collective purposes of work have trouble maintaining their daily routines and activities outside the workplace. Without the sense of purpose and the daily contact with others that work provides, nonwork life activities and pastimes become less meaningful and social interaction declines. In Marienthal, library loans declined by 50 percent over a two-year period despite the fact that all borrowing charges were dropped. Newspaper subscriptions were canceled even though they were offered at greatly reduced rates, and memberships in athletic and political clubs fell. As the social horizons of the unemployed receded, marital relations grew strained. Couples were thrown together for longer periods of unstructured time, and this domestic confinement generated conflict.

A related theme in studies of the unemployed, from the depression to the present day, is the effect of job loss upon social status and identity. The work role defines our place within the community, and the social esteem accorded that role shapes personal identity. Social standing and identity interlink to a degree that we are seldom aware of—until they change. Without a socially esteemed role in the community, the unemployed come to perceive of themselves as useless. They feel inadequate and their language reflects a sense of insignificance and worthlessness. Thus the residents of Marienthal often described themselves as "being on the scrap heap." Nearly everyone in Marienthal was unemployed, but these feelings can be just as intense when many community residents have jobs. In his depression-era study of Greenwich, Connecticut, E. Wright Bakke (1933) records an unemployed respondent as saying:

> [Y]ou are not human [when unemployed]. You're out of place. You're so different from all the rest of the people around that you think something is wrong with you. I don't care what your job is, you feel a lot more important when you come home at night than if you had been tramping around the streets all day. (cited in Jahoda 1982:24–25)

The loss of social standing and self-esteem that undermines the position of the unemployed within the community and in their own eyes is particularly destructive when it reinforces racial and ethnic stereotypes. In a contemporary ethnographic study of the displaced rubber workers of Barberton, Ohio, Greg Pappas (1989:79–82) gives a poignant example of the effect of job loss by telling the story of a forty-eight-year-old black man who was never able to find another job. Dependent upon his wife for support, he began to describe himself as a "lazy nigger who lies around while a woman supports him" and was eventually hospitalized for suicidal depression. The loss of the work role diminished his self-esteem and left him vulnerable to racist stereotypes. His inability to reject those stereotypes in his own mind ultimately became life threatening.

The work role provides the basis for the temporal organization and routines that give coherence and meaning to daily life; it sustains social contacts and interaction within the workplace and in nonwork life; and it confers social standing and a sense of self-worth. Many jobs may be so unsatisfying, so lowly valued, and so poorly rewarded that they add little or nothing to our lives. That fact does not diminish the importance of the work role in contemporary society. The underemployed, like the unemployed, have to create through their own efforts the sense of purpose and meaning that the employed often take for granted. When those efforts are not fully successful, when people who have internalized a work ethic are no longer able to contribute to society, they lose confidence in themselves and in social institutions. A common reaction to job loss is an erosion of trust and a high degree of cynicism regarding the motives of others. Carolyn and Robert

Perrucci and Dena and Harry Targ (1988) describe the loss of confidence in institutions and the weakened social integration of workers displaced by the closing of the RCA plant in Monticello, Indiana. Compared to a similar group of employed workers and to a national sample of Americans, the former RCA workers expressed less confidence in a wide range of institutions, especially those involving political and business leaders. Their alienation was not limited to specific situations, but extended outward from their suspicions about why the plant closed, to feelings of being ignored by the community, to beliefs in limited opportunities and in the need for radical social change.

The sizable fraction of the displaced work force who experience long jobless spells thus lose more than earnings. They experience psychological as well as material deprivation. The clinical evidence on the effects of long-term unemployment illustrates and substantiates this claim. The initial reaction to termination is often one of disbelief and anxiety. Many experience it as an emotional loss and go through the phases of the grieving process, including denial, anger, bargaining, and depression (Amondson and Borgen 1982; Hurst and Shepard 1986). As unemployment continues, people often experience levels of stress that imperil both physical health and psychological well-being. The unremitting stress of prolonged unemployment has been shown to be associated with high blood pressure and with high cholesterol and blood sugar levels, the risk factors for coronary heart disease, diabetes, and ulcers. The stress of job loss and unemployment is also associated with depression and suicidal behavior.[9]

The long-term unemployed eventually reach a point where their mood stabilizes and stress decreases, but they reach that point by becoming apathetic and by accepting their status as permanent. Instead of actively seeking to change their situation, they become passively resigned to it. They come to expect rejection as they lose faith in their ability to control their lives. In the process, they pass from being unemployed to being unemployable. We associate the resignation of the unemployed with the depression-era residents of Marienthal or with the plight of many of the poor today, but the psychological consequences of prolonged unemployment are similar, if less severe, for most people. Witness the complaint of a forty-six-year-old bank officer displaced during the recent recession:

> I have no career aspirations. I don't want to move up. At my age I'm not very hopeful about finding another good job. For me, the American Dream is dead. (cited in Labich 1993:40)

The psychological adjustment of the long-term unemployed is a response to the frustrations and disappointments of unsuccessful job search, but it also contributes to the ineffectiveness of that search. Long unemployment spells undermine self-confidence and motivation and stigmatize the job-seeker in the eyes of prospective employers who regard such spells as evidence of undesirable traits. The quote by the "large employer of labour" at the beginning of this chapter is from a report made by England's Charity Society in 1886. It shows that employers have long been aware of the detrimental effects of unemployment and have long been hesitant to hire the long-term jobless. Nearly half of the workers displaced in the United States over the past decade were out of work for at least three months. Hopefully, contemporary personnel managers are more sanguine about the effects of unemployment than this "large employer of labour," but it would be naive to assume that there is no bias against hiring the long- or even the medium-term unemployed. Prolonged jobless spells lessen the chances of being rehired because they are harmful, and because employers believe they are harmful. Freud ([1930] 1963) summarized the research on the effects of unemployment when he wrote that work is our strongest tie to reality and that by structuring experience it protects us from anxiety and emotion. Studies of the long-term unemployed, from the depression to the present day, confirm and elaborate upon his insight.

THE SOURCES OF LABOR MARKET DISADVANTAGE

With the exception of being born and (usually) of dying, there is an element of choice in everything we do and certainly in every decision we make. That fact should not distort our perception of the labor market or blind us to the obstacles and constraints that many job-seekers face. The lengthy jobless spells of most of those displaced during the past decade were not productive; they did not result in better job matches or increased earnings. For many, job loss meant economic dislocation.

The reemployment difficulties of displaced workers often begin with the collapse of demand for their skills and experience. They experience a decline in their earnings ability as labor market shifts devalue skills and eliminate high-wage jobs. The restricted job search of older and less-educated workers and the obstacles to reemployment encountered by women and racial minorities make adjusting to this earnings loss particularly difficult. When people cannot find jobs comparable to those they have lost, their commitment to work weakens. Many move into and out of the work force, experiencing lengthy jobless spells in the process. Over time, the disadvantages of obsolete skills and ineffective job search are compounded by the deprivations and stress of prolonged unemployment. Those who experience lengthy unemployment spells acquire stigma in the eyes of prospective employers and lose the motivation and self-confidence needed to engage in active search.

When only the monetary costs of displacement are considered, the process of adjusting to a job loss appears straightforward. Individuals improve their chances of reemployment by lowering their wage expectations. But when we consider the psychological meaning and importance of the work role, the process of adjusting to displacement appears more complicated. Greatly lowering one's expectations has a negative effect upon the self-concept and sense of personal efficacy and may actually diminish the chances of reemployment. Evidence of the adverse effects of unemployment can be found in the DWS. A consistent finding of those surveys is that the reemployment rate of displaced workers declines as their jobless spells continue.[10] The longer people remain out of work, the less likely they are to find new jobs at any given point in time. What makes this finding significant is that it is not explained by any observable characteristics of the long-term jobless. The chances of finding another job decline over time regardless of the personal characteristics or prior experience of the job-seeker. This decline in the reemployment rate could be the result of unobserved traits such as motivation that affect job search, but displaced workers are experienced workers whose ability and desire to work are evidenced by their prior employment history. In controlling for that history, we also control for the unobserved traits that contributed to their previous employment success. The employment histories in the DWS indicate that the duration of joblessness per se has a detrimental effect upon individuals and reduces their chances of reemployment.

These sources of labor market disadvantage explain why some individuals and groups are more likely than others to endure long jobless spells. But in the final analysis the efficacy of job search and the rate of unemployment depend upon the number of attractive jobs that are available. People remain out of work not just because their skills are obsolete, which they often are; or because they encounter obstacle to effective job search, which they often do; or even because they lose confidence in their ability to find and hold a job, which often happens. They remain unemployed because there are too few jobs that offer wages comparable to what they have been receiving or to what many similarly qualified workers still earn.

The problem is not a lack of employment growth nationwide, although many localities are economically depressed. The reemployment difficulties of most displaced workers have more to do with the kind of jobs being created than with their number. Nor is the problem one of unrealistic wage expectations. The employment histories of both the former Chrysler workers and the respondents to the DWS show that most displaced workers quickly accept lower real wage offers. What they are hesitant to accept are jobs that pay a fraction of their former wage. To understand why millions of workers are experiencing difficulty finding jobs that enable them to maintain their standard of living, we need to examine the economic trends that are giving rise to the turbulence within the labor market. The following chapters describe some of those trends and the challenge they pose for public policy.

NOTES

1.   Earnings analyses may not even capture the full economic costs of prolonged unemployment because the long-term jobless are underrepresented in the samples used to estimate earnings losses (see Moore 1990).

2.   Job search theories are surveyed in Lippmann and McCall (1976a, 1976b).

3.   Beginning with the 1988 survey, respondents were asked how many weeks went by before they started working again at another job, a continuous spell. The two earlier surveys asked how many weeks they were without work following displacement and may measure interrupted spells.

4.   In light of the change in question wording, the sharp decrease in this racial difference between the 1986 and 1988 surveys indicates that the jobless spells of many black workers are separated by intermittent periods of employment. If so, measuring joblessness as a single continuous spell underestimates the racial disparity in the chances for stable reemployment.

5.   This "spatial mismatch hypothesis" was originally presented in Kain (1968). For a review of the literature that followed Kain's article, see Holzer (1989).

6.   As was explained with regard to the figures in Table 2.4, the proportionate wage losses shown in Table 3.2 were estimated from the average log difference between the former and current weekly wage, after adjusting for inflation.

7.   Multivariate analysis of the 1984 and 1986 DWS indicates that the reemployment chances of blacks are less than half those of whites (Moore 1992; see also Podgursky and Swaim 1987b).

8.   This summary of the thematic findings of the Marienthal study follows Jahoda (1982:22–26).

9.   There is a huge literature on the physical and mental health effects of unemployment. A good introduction to this research is Cobb and Kasl (1977). The long-term effects of stress are also analyzed by Pearlin, Menaghan, Lieberman, and Mullin (1981).

10.   Event history analyses of the reemployment probabilities of displaced workers consistently show what is termed "negative duration dependence" (see Podgursky and Swaim 1987b; Moore 1992).

The Sources of Economic Dislocation _____ II

Productivity and Competitiveness 4

[I]t is simply not the case that the world's leading nations are to any important degree in economic competition with each other, or that any of their major economic problems can be attributed to failures to compete on world markets.

—Paul Krugman, "Competitiveness: A Dangerous Obsession."

In the years immediately following the Second World War the United States dominated the world economy. Its domestic market was eight times as large as that of Great Britain, the second leading industrial power. This huge domestic market provided unmatched economies of scale and kept the production costs of industry low. Its wealth, accumulated from over a century of exploiting an abundance of raw materials and land, sustained an absolute level of investment and an amount of capital per worker that was unmatched by any other nation (Dertouzos, Lester, and Solow, 1989:23–26). American productivity and incomes were the envy of the rest of the world.

Today, these advantages have largely disappeared. The relative decline of the U.S. economy can be seen in per capita income, the broadest measure of living standards. Income comparisons are complicated by national differences in the cost of living and in the provision of public services, but measured in terms of external purchasing power—the value of goods and services that can be bought if income is spent abroad—the per capita income of a growing number of industrial countries exceeds that of the United States. Much of this relative change can be attributed to the postwar recovery of other industrial economies and is a positive development. But over the past two decades the real earnings of production and nonsupervisory workers have fallen, real family incomes have stagnated, economic and social inequalities have worsened, and the threat of prolonged unemployment and earnings loss has eroded the security of individuals and families. These difficulties can be linked, directly or indirectly, to slower economic growth.

Many observers attribute our economic problems to a loss of U.S. competitiveness in world markets at a time when trade accounts for a growing share of economic activity. As the introductory quote indicates, this view is disputed. One of the leading authorities on international trade has openly challenged the commonly held belief that the world's industrial nations are in economic competition with one another, or that their economic problems can be attributed to a failure to compete on world markets. Although trade

53

accounts for a increasing share of economic activity, Paul Krugman (1994) points out that the rate of income growth both in this and other major industrial countries remains equal to the rate of domestic productivity growth. Over the long run, improvements in living standards depend upon the ability of each country to raise its output per worker.

Krugman can be criticized for minimizing the disruptive impact of world trade, but his views regarding the overriding importance of domestic productivity for wages and living standards are widely shared. In their 1989 report, *Made in America* (Dertouzos et al. 1989), the MIT Commission on Industrial Productivity concluded that this country has a serious productivity problem and that its low rate of productivity growth, relative both to other nations and to our own history, is rooted in "attitudinal and organizational weaknesses that pervade America's production system." The commission further determined that these weaknesses are the result of the way people and organizations interact, the way they deal with risk and, most importantly, the way they seek to develop and utilize human resources (Dertouzos et al. 1989:166). In other words, the causes of the slower economic growth that threatens the prosperity of American workers and families are largely internal.

Judged in terms of net job growth, the U.S. economy performed relatively well over the past two decades as millions of individuals entered the work force, but it has not been able to sustain both high employment and productivity growth during a period of rapid economic and technological change. The rate of productivity growth has slowed, and labor productivity is the basis of future prosperity. It creates the wealth out of which wages and salaries are paid. The specific causes of this slowdown are disputed, but there is no disagreement over its significance. Improving the earnings ability of the average worker will depend upon restoring productivity growth to its historic trend.

The increased affluence produced by productivity growth is valuable not only because it allows for higher standards of living, but also because it mediates social conflict. It makes it possible for some people to consume more without others consuming less. As living standards rise, the more affluent members of society become more willing to share with the less fortunate. But when growth slows, people try to preserve what they have and they show less concern for the poor. Slower productivity growth is therefore likely to mean greater distributional conflict and increased earnings and income inequality.

PRODUCTIVITY, EMPLOYMENT, AND INCOME GROWTH

The importance of productivity to economic welfare is perhaps best illustrated by means of the identities that define national output and per capita income. By definition, the growth of national output equals the growth in employment plus the growth in labor productivity:

output growth = employment growth + productivity growth

National output (i.e., gross domestic product, or GDP) increases either when the number of persons employed increases or when those who are employed produce more goods and services. A corollary definition equates the growth of per capita income to labor productivity growth plus any increase in the employment-to-population ratio (EPR), the proportion of the working-age population that is employed:

per capita income growth = growth of EPR + productivity growth

Per capita income rises either when the fraction of the population that is employed becomes larger or when those who are employed produce more. These identities simplify the actual measurement of output and income trends, which depend upon fluctuations in the number of hours worked. Nonetheless, they provide a framework for assessing the sources of economic growth over the past two decades.

Most of the growth of the U.S. economy since 1970 is due to the increasing size of the work force. The figures in Table 4.1 show that between 1970 and 1992 national output grew at an average annual rate of 2.6 percent a year. The same period saw the number of people employed increase by 1.8 percent a year. The annual increase in labor productivity during this period therefore averaged less than 1 percent. This contrasts with the experience of both Europe and Japan. The major European economies grew about as rapidly as the United States, but the number of people employed increased much more slowly. The long-term growth of Europe's major economies can

Table 4.1. Output and Employment Growth of Major Industrial Countries, 1970–92 (Average Annual Change)

Country	Output (%)[a]	Employment (%)	Employment-Population Ratio			
			1970	1989	1992	Change 1970–92[b]
U.S.	2.6	1.8	57.4	63.0	61.4	+4.0
Canada	3.1	2.0	54.5	62.0	58.1	+3.6
France	2.4	0.3	55.9	50.0	50.2	−5.7
Germany	2.5	0.4	56.5	51.8	52.9	−3.6
Italy	2.7	0.5	47.6	43.6	43.9	−3.7
U.K.	1.8	0.2	59.3	59.3	56.5	−2.8
Japan	4.1	1.1	63.8	60.8	62.0	−1.8

[a] Increase in real GDP.
[b] Percentage point change in employment to population ratio.
Sources: Monthly Labor Review, various years.

be attributed almost entirely to productivity gains. Japan's economy has grown more rapidly than ours because of the rapidly increasing productivity of a work force that grows about 1 percent a year.

A similar point can be made with regard to per capita income, which rose in the United States at a rate of less than 2 percent a year during this period. Much of this improvement in per capita income was due to the increasing percentage of the adult population who work. In 1970, a little over 57 percent of the U.S. adult population was employed. By 1989, the EPR had risen to 63 percent, before falling to 61.4 percent during the recent recession. Again, this contrasts with the demographic trends in other major industrial countries. With the exception of Canada, their employment ratios have declined since 1970. The labor force participation of men is decreasing in every major industrial country, while that of women is increasing. But the drop in the male participation rate has been more rapid in Europe than in this country, and the increase in female participation has been slower. A major reason for this difference is slower population growth. The populations of Germany, France, Italy, and the United Kingdom are all growing more slowly, and aging more rapidly, than those of the United States and Canada. The living standards of Europeans and Japanese improved primarily because they produced more goods and services without a large increase in the number of people who work.

The relationship between productivity, employment, and income clarifies some common misconceptions regarding job creation. In popular discussion the economic well-being of communities is closely linked to job growth. As discussed in Chapter 1, business and government officials justify local economic development efforts, and especially the use of business subsidies and locational incentives, in terms of the additional employment opportunities that they are thought to produce. Political campaigns often revolve around the promises of candidates to "create" more jobs, and one of the most damaging charges that can be leveled against an incumbent is that his or her term in office saw little or no employment gains. Unfortunately, the rhetoric of job creation that pervades local politics tends to overlook the importance of labor productivity to worker earnings. Millions of people, representing an increasing percentage of the working-age population, entered the labor force during the 1970s and 1980s, yet the real earnings of most workers fell. The prosperity of individuals and communities alike depends upon the kind as well as the number of new jobs.

The rhetoric of job creation also obscures the principal reason for employment growth. The number of people employed increased by nearly twenty-one million in the 1970s and by more than eighteen million in the 1980s because of the labor force entry of the baby-boom generation and the increasing participation of women. By the late 1980s the baby-boom was being followed by the baby-bust, the rate of female participation was leveling off, and the creation of new jobs had slowed dramatically. Widespread misunderstanding of the sources of employment growth affects national as well as local politics and sometimes even misleads those most responsible for perpetuating this misunderstanding. In his 1988 campaign, former president Bush appealed to voters by promising to create thirty million new jobs over the next eight years. His promise was consistent with the rate of job generation during the two preceding administrations, but it showed a very poor understanding of the social and demographic forces behind those job gains. As it turned out, there was little net employment growth during his one term in office.

Demographic trends help to explain Europe's slow employment growth over the past two decades. The adult population of major European countries is growing at less than half the U.S. rate. This slowly growing and more rapidly aging population limits both the supply of labor and the demand for the goods and services that labor produces. As a population ages and the number of labor market entrants decreases, real wages rise and firms hire fewer additional workers. A slowly growing population also constrains the demand for additional goods and services. Together, higher labor costs and the relatively small number of additional consumers act to slow job growth.

The crucial importance of social and demographic trends does not mean that the strength of the national economy has no effect upon employment. Unemployment rose throughout Europe in the 1980s as economic conditions worsened and labor demand weakened. The slower rate of job growth in many European countries has been termed "Eurosclerosis," characterized by an International Labor Office official as an "arthritic tightening of sinews, a virulent disease supposedly ravaging the boardrooms, union headquarters and government departments all over Europe" (quoted in Harrison and Bluestone 1988:112). The common diagnosis for this condition attributes the lack of employment growth to the constraints imposed upon employers by powerful unions and by social welfare and labor market policies, constraints that are less evident in the highly competitive U.S. labor market. It is fair to say that Europe's export-oriented economies have pursued rapid productivity growth at the cost of higher unemployment, but a balanced account of the reasons for high unemployment would highlight the role of the region's most powerful central bank. Expecting West Germany's work force to shrink, and fearful that rapid economic growth would lead to the importation of millions of additional "guest" workers, the Bundesbank adhered to restrictive monetary policies during the 1980s.[1] The result was slower growth and higher unemployment throughout Europe, yet the policies that helped to produce higher unemployment were adopted in response to projected demographic trends. The reunification of Germany in 1989 may have eliminated the demographic bottleneck, but fear of the inflationary effects of unification continue to keep interest rates high and employment growth rates low.

The point is that cross-national comparisons of employment growth, like the job creation rhetoric used to promote local economic development, can be misleading. Over the long term, social and demographic trends determine the level of employment, and increasing the number of people employed does not assure improved living standards. The benefits of prosperity ultimately depend upon the productivity part of the identities that define output and income growth. It is possible to raise income and consumption levels for a while by putting a larger fraction of the population to work, as we have done. But there are obvious limits to this, and it is doubtful that the EPR will continue to rise as the American population ages and the participation rate of women approaches that of men. It is also possible to increase consumption by running a trade deficit and then borrowing, or selling assets, to cover that deficit, as we also have done. But since the borrowing must eventually stop and the debts must be repaid, foreign borrowing raises present consumption only by creating claims upon future income. The only sustainable way to increase per capita income is to raise the productivity of the average worker.

THE PRODUCTIVITY SLOWDOWN

Labor productivity is defined as the value of output per hour worked in the business sector of the economy although the Bureau of Labor Statistics actually measures output per hour paid. It is also sometimes measured as output per person employed. Whichever definition is used, productivity matters because of its link to real income and earnings. Productivity growth raises real income by reducing prices. In some industries, output gains lead directly to higher wages, but under competitive conditions higher productivity usually translates into lower labor costs and lower prices. Consumers benefit because lower prices raise their real incomes. The classic example of this process is agriculture. Labor productivity in agriculture has increased much faster than in the economy as a whole, yet the earnings of agricultural workers have not risen relative to those of workers in other sectors (Council of Economic Advisors 1988:68). Rather, the relative prices of agricultural goods have fallen. Few industries are as competitive as agriculture, but the basic point still holds. Productivity growth raises living standards by increasing the purchasing power and real income of consumers.

In light of the connection between productivity gains and real income, the figures in Table 4.2 merit concern. Over the quarter-century ending in 1973, output per hour within the private nonfarm business sector rose at an average annual rate of 2.4 percent.[2] Since then, it has increased at no more than half that rate. Productivity growth began to slow in the mid-1960s, and it almost stopped during the 1970s. Between 1973 and 1981 productivity

Table 4.2.   U.S. Productivity Growth (%), 1948–93 (Average Annual Change)

	1948–73	1973–81	1981–93
Business sector	2.9	0.6	1.3
Nonfarm business	2.4	0.5	1.2
Manufacturing	2.8	1.3	2.8

Sources: Monthly Labor Review, various years.

increased at an annual rate of 0.5 percent, and it has grown at a rate of only 1.2 percent a year since then. The recent productivity record thus compares badly not only with that of other major industrial countries, but also with our own history.

The one bright spot in this picture is the apparent recovery of manufacturing productivity in the 1980s. However, Baily and Chakrabarti (1988:5–7) argue that the gains within manufacturing may be overstated for several reasons. First, much of the improvement is due to the performance of a single industry: computers. Second, the recession and high value of the dollar during the first half of the decade forced the closing of less-efficient plants, resulting in one-time productivity gains. The increase in manufacturing productivity was achieved in large part by reducing capacity and displacing millions of workers, not by building more efficient plants. Finally, government analysts measure output for the economy as a whole and then allocate growth to each industry sector, a procedure that tends to overstate manufacturing gains.[3] Whatever the reasons for the apparent recovery, it did not extend to the rest of the economy. The rate of productivity growth remains at historically low levels for the private sector as a whole.

Identifying the causes of this slowdown has proved difficult. Labor productivity can increase for two distinct reasons: either because more capital is used per worker or because the production process incorporates technical change and better management practices. The contribution from improved technology and management is called multifactor productivity and is not directly observed or measured. Rather, it is calculated by subtracting from total output the contributions from increased amounts of capital and labor. Whatever is not explained by the measured inputs to production is attributed to multifactor productivity and is assumed to reflect increased efficiency in the use of labor and capital resources.[4] Technological advance, improvements in the education and skills of the work force, better management techniques, reorganization of the production process, all of these and more contribute to multifactor productivity.

The figures in Table 4.3 are based upon the work of Alicia Munnell, an economist at the Federal Reserve Bank of Boston. They show the different sources of labor productivity growth in the nonfarm business sector between

1948 and 1987. As the table reveals, output per hour slowed from 2.5 percent a year before 1969 to only 1.1 percent thereafter, yet the contribution of capital to labor productivity remained constant. The rates of growth in the capital-labor ratio during the two periods are identical, and capital's contribution to productivity grew at an average annual rate of 0.7 percent in both periods. The slowdown in productivity growth thus appears to be due solely to the decline in multifactor productivity.[5]

Measured as a residual, multifactor productivity is not directly observed and is therefore subject to varying interpretation. Nobody knows exactly what accounts for it or why it would decline, but measuring the contribution of the capital and labor inputs to production does rule out some of the common explanations for slower growth. For example, the timing of the slowdown and the apparent recovery of manufacturing productivity coincide with the oil price shocks of the 1970s and the subsequent decline in energy prices in the 1980s. The rise in energy prices resulted in the premature obsolescence of some plant and equipment, but there is no decline in the growth of capital investment during this period because energy is too small an input to production to explain more than a small fraction of the decline (Gullickson and Harper, 1987). Government regulatory policies and the diversion of capital into "nonproductive" uses such as pollution abatement could have slowed the flow of capital services without any dropoff in the amount of capital investment, but recent studies find little support for this argument either (see Baily and Chakrabarti, 1988).

A different set of explanations for the slowdown focus upon the rapid growth of the work force after 1969. The labor force entry of large numbers of inexperienced workers could depress productivity in a couple of ways. First, any rapid increase in labor supply tends to keep wages low, and lower real wages mean firms have less incentive to invest in labor-saving equipment and technology. This explains part of the slowdown in those indus-

Table 4.3. Sources of Productivity Growth in Private Nonfarm Business, 1948–87 (Average Annual Change)

Period	Output per hour	Multi-factor productivity	Contribution of Capital		
			Capital-labor ratio	Capital's share	Contribution to output per hour
1948–69	2.5	1.8	2.1	.356	.7
1969–87	1.1	.4	2.1	.348	.7
1969–73	2.0	1.1	2.7	.345	.9
1973–79	.5	−.1	1.7	.347	.6
1979–87	1.2	.4	2.2	.348	.8

Source: Munnell (1990, table 1).

tries, predominantly in the service sector, where employment grew most rapidly. Investment in physical capital did not keep pace with the growth of employment, and Table 4.3 shows that capital's contribution to productivity in the nonfarm business sector fell slightly during the 1973–79 period. Still, most of the slowdown is clearly the result of a decline in multifactor productivity; it is not explained by changes in the capital-labor ratio.

A second way in which rapid employment growth could depress productivity is by changing the demographic composition and experience level of the work force. Inexperienced workers are less efficient, and although the effect was small, the entry of millions of younger and less experienced workers slowed growth somewhat during the 1970s. Munnell (1990:11) estimates that the changing age-sex mix of the work force accounted at most for 0.2 of the 1.4 percentage point decline in multifactor productivity. Moreover, by 1980 the experience level of the work force had begun to rise. If the increase in the fraction of younger and less experienced workers contributed initially to the slowdown, the reversal of that trend should have raised productivity throughout the 1980s.

In short, the productivity slowdown cannot be attributed to changes in the capital-labor ratio or to the changing size and composition of the work force. Recent attempts to move beyond these traditional explanations have identified several new culprits. Baily and Chakrabarti (1988) attribute our slow productivity growth to the rate of technical innovation. They argue that raising productivity depends primarily upon the diffusion and refinement of known technologies, and the United States has been slow to incorporate existing knowledge into production. The problem is not that technological opportunities have declined, but that available opportunities have been missed. A somewhat different explanation is offered by Aschauer (1989) in a very provocative article that traced the slowdown to the near cessation of investment in public infrastructure. The growth of output in the private sector depends upon the stock of public capital as well as the amount of private capital, and the level of public investment has declined sharply in this country. As a result, the deterioration and crowding of roads, bridges, and other transportation links has increased the cost of producing and distributing goods and services. Building upon this thesis, Munnell (1990) attributes much of the drop in multifactor productivity to the omission of public capital from the calculation of inputs to production. Finally, Barry and Irving Bluestone (1992) emphasize the deterioration of labor-management relations and the general failure of our industrial relations system to foster productivity gains, improved product quality, and more rapid innovation.

These explanations, among others, highlight different aspects of the slowdown. Although there is no consensus on the specific causes of slower growth, the work of these analysts supports some general conclusions. The productivity crisis cannot be explained in terms of the amount of private capital and other inputs to production. Rather, it represents a failure to make better use of our human and other resources. That failure reflects a lack of understanding of the importance of the public sector to economic growth, and reversing the productivity decline will require greater investment in public goods, including worker training. Making better use of existing resources also means better management, and that depends upon the stability and character of employer-employee relations.

THE TRADE DEFICIT AND THE COMPETITIVENESS DEBATE

The image of industrial workers losing their jobs as factories close or relocate has been deeply imprinted upon the national consciousness. That image raises fears that the country is losing its industrial base and that the employment and earnings losses of displaced workers reflect the growing inability of U.S. industry to compete in international markets at a time when trade represents a rapidly increasing share of economic activity. While these fears are understandable, they may be misdirected. The rise of international trade during the 1970s was the proximate cause of the competitive difficulties of many domestic industries, but the expansion of trade need not have resulted in slower growth or reduced employment and earnings opportunities. Countries that maintain strong productivity growth see the relative prices of their goods decline on world markets. A more open economy should mean increased demand for the goods they produce and higher incomes for the workers who produce them. The ability to compete in international markets ultimately depends upon a nation's productivity growth.

In a shrinking world it is inevitable that trade will account for a growing share of all the major industrial economies. Between 1961 and 1981 the volume of world merchandise trade increased 50 percent faster than manufacturing output (Office of Technology Assessment 1986:372). More and more of the world's production is being exported, and more and more of its consumption is being imported. The expanded role of trade within the U.S. economy became evident after 1970 and coincided with the productivity slowdown. The value of merchandise trade increased from 8.2 percent of GDP in that year to 16.4 percent in 1993. Relative to the size of the economy, the importance of merchandise trade doubled.

Unfortunately, the expansion of this trade has not been balanced: imports have increased more rapidly than exports. The figures in Table 4.4 show that the U.S. merchandise trade balance turned negative in 1971. By the late 1970s the imbalance amounted to about 1 percent of GDP each year as American industry was unable to offset growing oil imports with expanded exports. Following the recession of 1980–82 the trade gap widened dramat-

Table 4.4.   U. S. Merchandise Trade Balance, 1970–93

Year	Billion $	% GDP	Year	Billion $	% GDP
1970	2.7	0.3	1982	−31.8	−1.1
1971	−2.0	−0.2	1983	−57.5	−2.0
1972	−6.4	−0.6	1984	−107.9	−3.0
1973	1.3	0.1	1985	−132.1	−3.0
1974	−4.5	−0.4	1986	−152.7	−3.6
1975	9.1	0.6	1987	−152.1	−3.4
1976	−8.3	−0.5	1988	−118.6	−2.6
1977	−29.2	−1.5	1989	−109.6	−2.1
1978	−31.1	−1.5	1990	−101.7	−1.8
1979	−27.6	−1.2	1991	−65.4	−1.1
1980	−24.2	−0.9	1992	−84.3	−1.4
1981	−27.3	−0.9	1993	−115.8	−1.8

Source: Statistical Abstract of the United States, various years.

ically, growing to more than 3 percent of GDP. Although the trade deficit relative to the size of the economy decreased after 1986, the gap between imports and exports has remained large, averaging well over on hundred billion dollars a year.

As a general proposition, a merchandise trade surplus means greater demand for manufactured goods and for the workers who produce those goods, while a trade deficit means the opposite. Any trade imbalance therefore represents a potential job loss, and the connection between this trade deficit and the loss of well-paying manufacturing jobs is of particular concern. Apart from the sizable fraction of the work force that it still employs, manufacturing supports high-wage jobs in engineering and design, accounting, finance, insurance, and other business and legal services. Fully one-quarter of GDP consists of services that are closely linked to manufacturing, and the loss of domestic production jeopardizes these ancillary services and the jobs they provide (Cohen and Zysman 1987:22). Nor can we count upon the export of services to pay for the goods that we import. The value of manufactured imports is many times that of the services we export, and the trade in services offsets only a small part of the merchandise deficit. The trade imbalance is also a matter of concern, apart from its impact upon potential employment, because it mortgages our future prosperity. It raises present consumption only by creating claims upon future income.[6]

Despite these negative aspects of the trade imbalance, there is little agreement regarding the causes of the deficit or its role in actual manufacturing job losses. The Council of Economic Advisors (CEA) under Presidents Reagan and Bush blamed the trade deficit upon an adverse macroeconomic environment and the flawed monetary and fiscal policies that produced that environment. They saw no evidence of long-term industrial decline in manufacturing output and employment trends (e.g., CEA 1988:176–79). Other observers have been less sanguine. Although the issues involved are complex, examining the disagreements between the CEA and its critics helps to clarify some of the consequences of slower economic growth.

Consistent with the conservative agenda of the Reagan and Bush administrations, the CEA attributed the competitive difficulties of U.S. firms to the effect of the tax system upon the national savings rate and to the effect of monetary policy upon interest rates. The low savings rate in this country and the comparatively high cost of capital were blamed for adversely affecting the level of investment and the competitive performance of firms. The monetary policies of the Federal Reserve Board were particularly important in this regard. With inflation running at over 12 percent by the late 1970s, the Federal Reserve raised interest rates sharply and precipitated the worst recession in the postwar period. Higher interest rates increase the price of everything bought on credit, so the demand for new homes and cars and other durable goods declined. At the same time, higher interest rates raised the borrowing costs of U.S. firms well above what most foreign firms had to pay in their credit markets, and new business investment also decreased. Finally, higher interest rates attracted foreign investors and drove up the value of the dollar on foreign exchange markets. American goods became more expensive, and therefore less competitive, on world markets.

By 1982 the impact of the recession had lowered inflation to under 4 percent, but huge government budget deficits kept interest rates high. Although the CEA was somewhat restrained when it came to criticizing the fiscal policies of the Reagan administration, it is now clear that the 1981 tax cut, combined with increased defense spending and the growth of entitlements, resulted in budget deficits that added more than a trillion dollars to the national debt before Reagan left office.[7] Because domestic savings were insufficient to finance these budget deficits and meet new investment demand, real interest rates rose to historically unprecedented levels. These real interest rates (about 5 percent above inflation) attracted the foreign capital needed to finance the budget deficit, but they also contributed to the trade deficit by driving the foreign-exchange value of the dollar even higher.

To understand how this happened it is necessary to realize that investment in the United States requires dollars. Foreigners can get dollars in exchange for either their currencies or their goods. When their demand for dollars exceeds our demand for their currency, they have to sell more goods to us (imports) than we sell to them (exports). This demand imbalance is usually corrected through the foreign exchange markets. With high interest rates attracting foreign investors, the exchange value of the dollar rose by 64 percent between 1980 and 1985 (Friedman 1989:182). Because U.S. exports are priced in dollars, they became less competitive in world markets just as imports became more affordable for American consumers. We imported more goods than we sold abroad, and foreigners acquired the dollars needed to invest in the United States. The value of the dollar thus regulated the foreign capital flows needed to finance massive government borrowing, adding in the process to the merchandise trade deficit.

In addition to assigning the trade imbalance to an unfavorable macro-economic environment, the CEA took issue with those who saw evidence of long-term industrial decline in manufacturing output and employment trends. Contrary to the belief that the United States is "deindustrializing," the CEA claimed that manufacturing output, measured in constant dollars, is expanding in measure with the overall growth of the economy and that it continues to account for about a quarter of the GDP. They also saw no evidence of industrial decline in manufacturing employment trends. Any actual job loss was assumed to result from fluctuations in labor demand and from rapid productivity gains. Most of the decline in manufacturing employ-ment that occurred during the early 1980s was attributed to the sharp drop in domestic demand during the 1980–82 recession. Following the reces-sion, demand picked up and output increased while manufacturing employ-ment remained flat. Yet as long as manufacturing output represents a constant share of an expanding economy, the absence of employment growth must be the result of rapid productivity gains. A 1988 report by the CEA summarizes this argument:

> Except for business cycle fluctuations, the shares of real manufacturing output and real final goods output have been remarkably stable. While manufactur-ing's share of employment has declined . . . this trend does not suggest any long-term weakness in the manufacturing sector. Instead, it reflects stronger productivity growth. (cited in Mishel 1989:36)

This conclusion may be overly optimistic. Correcting for what he con-siders to be errors in the way the government estimates sectoral output, Lawrence Mishel (1989:40–41) reports that manufacturing's share of total output actually fell by 3.2 percentage points between 1973 and 1987. This output loss represented three million potential manufacturing jobs, which is approximately the size of the employment loss attributed to the trade defi-cit.[8] The fact of the matter is that nobody knows precisely what the employ-ment impact of the trade deficit has been. But if manufacturing's share of total output has declined, then that output loss is partly responsible for the drop in manufacturing employment.

Furthermore, flawed monetary and fiscal policies gave rise to the huge trade deficits of the early to mid-1980s, but those policy failures do not explain the gradual erosion of the trade balance that can be traced back to the 1960s. Macroeconomic policy does not explain our inability, unlike Japan and Germany, to offset increased oil imports with a surplus of manu-factured exports. We imported more than we exported long before the federal budget deficits led to massive foreign borrowing. Nor can we blame the persistence of the trade deficit since the mid-1980s upon an overvalued dollar. The exchange value of the dollar began to decline in 1985 and has since fallen to postwar lows against major foreign currencies. Yet the merchandise trade gap, which peaked in 1986 at $155.7 billion, still amounted to more than $115 billion in 1993. Given the decline in interest rates and the falling value of the dollar, it is increasingly difficult to blame the trade deficit on an unfavorable macroeconomic environment. Deficiencies in product quality, in service to customers, and in new product development have also played a major role in the competitive difficulties of U.S. firms (Dertouzos et al. 1989).

As much as anything else, the trade deficit is symptomatic of the way in which many U.S. firms are choosing to compete. In the best of cases, firms respond to heightened competition with technological and organizational innovations that yield labor-saving productivity gains. They maintain their domestic output at the expense of domestic employment. As is too often the case, jobs are simply exported through subcontracting arrangements with foreign producers or through the movement of production facilities offshore. U.S. firms are much more likely than those of other countries to move production operations abroad, and this movement offshore is motivated by more than the need to gain access to foreign markets. The provisions of the U.S. tariff code allow companies to export parts and materials and then reimport finished products, paying duty only upon the value added by low-wage assembly operations. These so-called 806/807 imports have grown rapidly and by the early 1980s represented one-sixth of all manufactured imports (Office of Technology Assessment 1986:32).

The trade imbalance is thus due in part to American corporations making or assembling things abroad and then shipping them to the U.S. market. This practice accounts for a large portion of the trade deficit with Taiwan, Mexico, Singapore, South Korea, and even Japan. Of course, relocating production facilities offshore does little to raise the productivity of American workers. The more successful firms are at moving production offshore and at curbing domestic wage growth, the less incentive they have to invest in labor-saving technology, worker training, and new forms of work organization. The irony of the situation is that the concern over competitiveness is often used to justify the shift of production operations to low-wage sites outside our borders.

In summary, the macroeconomic policies of recent administrations greatly exacerbated the trade imbalance and are responsible for the loss of millions of jobs. But viewed over the long term, it is difficult to see how competitiveness means anything different than productivity growth. Obscured by the fluctuations in the foreign-exchange value of the dollar, the terms of trade have worsened. The value of the dollar required to maintain external balance has declined because the value of the goods we export has decreased relative to that of the goods we import (Baily and Chakrabarti 1988). The only way to reverse this trend is to improve the productivity of the American worker. If competitiveness is defined as the growth of U.S. productivity relative to that of other major industrial countries, there is reason for concern about long-run decline.

THE CHANGING PREREQUISITES OF PRODUCTIVITY GROWTH

The United States became a rich country because a relatively small population was free to exploit a natural environment that offered an abundance of raw materials and farm land. Today, neither those natural resources nor the accumulation of physical wealth assure continued prosperity. Only a few percent of the work force engage in agriculture and mining, and the production of agricultural goods and raw materials accounts for a declining share of GDP. Nor will investing our wealth in standard production technologies assure high-wage employment or rising living standards to American workers because those technologies are available to low-wage countries around the globe. Technological advances in transportation and communication have opened the world to trade and domestic markets to foreign producers. At least 70 percent of U.S. industry is now exposed to foreign competition (CEA 1985:346). Moreover, as incomes rise both here and abroad, mass markets tend to become niche markets where the concern for quality makes it difficult to compete through long production runs of standardized goods. The production of lower-quality goods that compete primarily on the basis of price is shifting to countries with lower-cost labor.

Producing high-quality goods for increasingly fragmented and competitive markets is only part of the challenge facing the major industrial economies. Less than 20 percent of the U.S. work force is employed in manufacturing, and this percentage will continue to decline. More than three-quarters of all workers are employed in the service sector, and the productivity of most of these workers is low. Raising the earnings ability of people who neither make nor move goods is also part of the challenge facing the United States and other industrial countries.

Meeting that challenge will require a greater investment in worker training and less hierarchical forms of work organization. In both manufacturing and service industries, productivity and quality gains depend increasingly upon the ability to innovate and to make continuous improvements in the work process. Yet without skilled and motivated workers, the time needed to introduce new technologies lengthens and costs increase. Innovation also thrives in an environment that allows for continuous learning and decentralized decision-making. Workers have to be able to use their judgment and to make decisions, and they need to be given authority for a wide range of tasks, rather than being confined to routinized job assignments.

To foster innovation and learning, the workplace must be reorganized. That reorganization should involve more than the elimination of hierarchy, and it should benefit the work force as a whole and not just the core employees of restructured firms. Peter Drucker (1993:90–96), one of this country's leading management analysts, argues that the key to improved productivity, particularly within service organizations, is the "concentration of job and task." Recalling Frederick Taylor's principles of scientific management, Drucker advocates the elimination of all activities that do not contribute to performance. In practice, this means contracting out any activities that do not fit into the organization's value system or lead to promotion into senior management. He supports this position with numerous examples of highly effective organizations that not only outsource maintenance and clerical work, but also contract for specialized services such as drafting, design, and library research.

The management effort to restructure organizations around their core functions is being driven by the need to make their employees more productive. It is an attempt to create less hierarchical organizations that employ fewer people because they only do work that is focused upon the organization's mission. However, restructuring has consequences that extend beyond the firm: it also affects the earnings and employment security of the workers who provide noncore services. The agencies that employ these workers provide some career opportunities, but for the most part they offer only a series of dead-end jobs. Outsourcing thus results in widespread displacement and contributes to the mushrooming growth of both temporary help agencies and the contingent work force. It raises the productivity of some employees while undermining the employment stability, and motivation, of many others. Yet the success of efforts to achieve faster growth will ultimately depend upon the opportunities available to all employees. Workers who are valued by their employers, who sense a mutual commitment to the employment relationship, exhibit greater motivation and effort in their work. If our goal is to reverse the productivity slowdown, then organizational changes should be judged for how well they promote continuous learning and meaningful career opportunities for the work force as a whole.

Finally, increased investment in worker training will require a more widely shared understanding and appreciation of the positive role of government. Markets do not function properly in the absence of any regulatory authority, and this is particularly true with regard to education and worker training. Without public subsidies and sanctions, employers will resist investing in the general skills of their workers for fear of increased turnover, and individuals will have little incentive to acquire training for which they may never be compensated. Education and training investments also benefit society in ways additional to the higher-value production and the higher earnings that accrue to employers and workers, and markets always underinvest in goods that yield positive externalities, or third-party benefits. We cannot assume, therefore, that market incentives are sufficient to produce the skills needed by a dynamic economy, and we should not regard investments in training as solely an individual responsibility.

NOTES

1. The role of the Bundesbank in Europe's slow employment growth is discussed in Thurow (1992:72–73).

2. Productivity gains within the business sector as a whole are affected by the movement of labor from farming to industry. Focusing upon the nonfarm sector minimizes the effect of this sectoral shift.

3. Apart from the difficulty of measuring manufacturing output, there is reason to be skeptical about the employment figures used to calculate productivity trends. A recent survey of the companies that supply temporary help found that as many as 425,000 workers were leased to manufacturing establishments at the end of 1992. These individuals are not counted as factory workers, and they are not included in the Labor Department's calculation of manufacturing output per hour worked. As a productivity expert at the department's Bureau of Labor Statistics acknowledged, "It appears that we are underestimating the growth in hours worked and overestimating the growth in productivity" (cited in Uchitelle 1993a).

4. Munnell (1990:5) shows how both concepts of productivity—labor productivity and multifactor productivity—are derived from the traditional production function. Expressed in terms of percentage growth over time, the production function equates the growth in output to the growth in multifactor productivity plus the weighted average of the increase in capital and labor inputs, where the weights s_K and s_L equal the relative importance of the two factors in the costs of production:

$$Q \text{ growth} = \text{MFP growth} + s_K K \text{ growth} + s_L L \text{ growth}$$

Subtracting the growth rate of labor from both sides of the equation (and recalling that a difference in growth rates equals the rate of growth of the ratio of two variables) yields the definition of labor productivity growth:

$$Q \text{ growth} - L \text{ growth} = \text{MFP growth} + s_K(K \text{ growth} - L \text{ growth})$$

Labor productivity is the sum of multifactor productivity plus the change in the capital-labor ratio weighted to reflect capital's share in total output.

5. Munnell's findings are not unique. Using a very different methodology, Gullickson and Harper (1987) found that the slower growth in manufacturing's hourly output after 1973 was due to a decline in multifactor productivity, and Dean and Kunze (1988) extended their analysis to the private sector as a whole. Edward Denison (1985), the dean of American productivity analysts, was also unable to account for most of the slowdown even after controlling for a wide variety of measured factors.

6.   We can always reduce the trade deficit by allowing the foreign exchange value of the dollar to fall, by going into recession, or by raising protectionist trade barriers, but all of these measures will lower the standard of living.

7.   The effects of the Reagan administration's fiscal policy upon the trade imbalance are analyzed in Friedman (1989) and Calleo (1992).

8.   The U.S. International Trade Commission (1986) estimates that every billion dollars of the trade deficit represents the loss of twenty-five thousand potential jobs, mostly in manufacturing, a loss that amounted to three million jobs by 1984.

More jobs aren't enough, we have to raise incomes.

—President Bill Clinton

The slowdown in economic growth has had a profound impact upon the living standards of American workers and their families. Changes in per capita income, the broadest measure of the standard of living, capture only part of that impact. Per capita income does not measure earnings inequality, and the earnings distribution has become more unequal. Per capita income also includes interest and dividends, rents, and capital gains. These returns to capital and land are concentrated in a very small percentage of the population, and unlike wages and salaries, they have risen appreciably in recent years. The economic welfare of the vast majority of Americans depends primarily upon the level and distribution of worker earnings, and both changed for the worse in the 1970s.

The overall earnings pattern is one of sluggish growth and increased inequality. The average real wage stagnated after 1973, a clear indicator of the productivity slowdown. By the late 1970s the earnings distribution was becoming much less equal as well. The combination of rising earnings inequality and slow earnings growth means that lower-paid Americans suffered substantial income losses. Underlying these trends are changes in the labor market that have shifted opportunities in favor of the more educated and skilled. Less-educated men, especially younger men, saw their real wages decline while the earnings of college graduates rose. The deteriorating fortunes of less-educated Americans are only partly explained by shifts in the kind of jobs and skills in demand. Shifts in labor demand have been similar across all advanced economies, yet only in the United States have the real wages of less-educated and lower-paid workers fallen (Freeman 1994). Labor market institutions and the sharp decline in union power have also contributed to the growth of wage inequality and to the real earnings losses of low-wage workers in this country.

What happens to individuals in the labor market inevitably affects families. The median family income has risen only very slowly over the past twenty years, despite the increased labor force participation of family members, and family income inequalities have worsened. As the income gap that

71

separates American families widens around a slowly growing average, living standards deteriorate. For more than a quarter-century following World War II the rich got richer but the poor got richer too, and the income distribution remained fairly stable. Since the late 1970s not only have the rich gotten richer and the poor poorer, but also the percentage of the population that is well-off has grown, and the fraction that is living in poverty has grown as well. Evidence of this inegalitarian trend can be found in the data from federal tax returns. Between 1980 and 1989, the number of working poor increased by roughly two million, while the number of taxpayers reporting incomes of a half-million dollars or more rose from 16,881 to 183,240, more than a tenfold increase (Bartlett and Steele 1992:4).

The increased inequality among American workers and families represents a net loss of social welfare because an extra dollar of income has a greater effect upon the living standards of the poor than it has upon those of the rich. Stated differently, real income losses diminish the welfare of the poor more than comparable income gains enhance the well-being of the rich. In the absence of rapid economic growth, a more unequal society is a poorer society. It is also a more divided society. Any change in the income distribution becomes a zero-sum game in which the gains of one group mean losses for others.

STAGNANT EARNINGS GROWTH

Measuring the trends in real earnings is complicated by the fluctuations of the business cycle, by the growing share of fringe benefits in total compensation, and by the changing demographic characteristics of the work force. There is no question that real hourly wage growth stagnated after 1973. Average hourly earnings (in 1982 dollars) of production and nonsupervisory workers fell from $8.55 in 1973 to $7.69 in 1981. This hourly wage then remained fairly stable throughout the 1980s before dropping to $7.39 by 1993, an overall decline of nearly 14 percent. The real weekly earnings of these workers declined even more steeply, partly as a result of the expanding use of part-time employment. Falling from a little over $315 in 1973 to less than $255 in 1993, real weekly wages dropped almost 20 percent (Council of Economic Advisors 1993, table B-42). These wage data exclude employer-provided benefits such as pensions and health insurance that represent a growing share of total compensation, and they are not based upon all employees. But no matter how we measure earnings growth, we arrive at the same general conclusion. After increasing rapidly for a quarter century following the Second World War, real earnings growth has stagnated.

Economists Frank Levy and Richard Murnane (1992:1337) demonstrate what slower earnings growth means by tracing the median individual income of year-round, full-time, male workers between the ages of forty-five and fifty-four over a forty-year period. Looking at a single age cohort of workers employed full-time minimizes the earnings fluctuations due to business cycles and to the changing age composition of the work force. The median income (in 1988 dollars) of this cohort of older males nearly doubled between 1948 and 1973, rising from $16,702 to $31,862. During the next 15 years, their real median income increased by less than $900. Adjusting for the cost of fringe benefits made little difference. Median income rose from $17,000 in 1948 to $34,074 in 1973, and then to $35,943 in 1988. The lack of improvement in the earnings ability of this cohort after 1973 testifies to the effects of slower economic growth.

Changes in the industry composition of employment account for a large part of these earnings trends. In an efficiently operating economy, without major obstacles to capital and labor mobility, the shift of employment from one industry to another is not supposed to affect wage levels. Equally productive workers should be compensated equally across industry sectors. However, this competitive ideal does not always describe the real world. There are large and persistent differences in industry wage levels, and the shift of employment from manufacturing to retail trade and service industries has affected the earnings ability of comparable workers.[1] It has also raised fears that the domestic economy is progressively less capable of generating well-paying jobs.

A study done for the Joint Economic Committee of the Congress by Robert Costrell showed that these fears have some basis in fact. Costrell examined the impact of industry employment shifts upon worker compensation over a series of time periods stretching from 1947 to 1987.[2] For each period he calculated the average total compensation in industries with a decreasing, or contracting, share of total employment as well as in industries with an increasing, or expanding, employment share. For the years 1981 through 1986 he found that the difference in compensation had increased dramatically. The wages and benefits of the jobs lost in contracting industries amounted, on average, to approximately ten thousand dollars a year more than the wages and benefits of the jobs being created in expanding industries. He also found that the rate at which employment was shifting from contracting to expanding industries had accelerated during this period.

These industry employment shifts have had a particularly adverse effect upon the earnings of production and nonsupervisory workers. The figures in Table 5.1 show the average weekly wage of production workers in both expanding and contracting industries for the periods 1972 to 1981 and 1981 to 1986. The industry wage gap more than doubled between these periods, increasing from about $65 to nearly $135, while the rate at which employment was shifting to lower-wage industries accelerated. Together, the widening wage gap and the quickening pace of employment change reduced

Table 5.1. Industry Employment Shifts and Production Worker Weekly Wages, 1972–86 (1987 Dollars)

	Rate of structural shift[a]	*Weekly wage*		*Shift effect on wage growth*
		Expanding industries	*Contracting industries*	
1981–86	1.46	287.51	422.20	−0.61
1972–81	1.23	295.65	361.13	−0.24

[a] Annual change in industry employment shares in percentage points.
Source: Robert Costrell, "The Effects of Industry Employment Shifts on Wage Growth, 1948–87," Joint Economic Committee, U.S. Congress, August 1988, reproduced in Mishel (1989, table 4).

wage growth by about six-tenths of a percentage point a year, and total compensation growth by three-quarters of a percentage point a year. Costrell estimates that at least half of this reduction was due to the loss of jobs in trade-sensitive durable-goods industries, and an additional 40 percent was the result of the employment growth in retail trade (Mishel 1989, pp 42-43). Most of the stagnation in worker earnings may be the result of anemic productivity gains within an expanding service sector, but Costrell's findings indicate that the loss of manufacturing jobs has also depressed earnings growth. As we shall see, these employment shifts have undermined the earnings ability of less-educated males in particular.

THE RISE IN EARNINGS INEQUALITY

Earnings growth and earnings inequality are distinct phenomena, but they combine in their effect upon wage earners. When earnings inequality increases around a stationary average, those at the bottom experience absolute as well as relative losses, while those at the top still enjoy real earnings gains. By the end of the 1980s it was clear that earnings inequality was increasing due to the growing disparity in wage rates. The distribution of wage earners resembled a wave, its forward motion stopped, that has begun to flatten. As the middle of the wave collapsed, the number of wage earners in the tails grew correspondingly larger.

The forces behind this inegalitarian trend operate on both sides of the labor market. The shift of employment out of manufacturing has contributed to wage inequality, but demographic changes in the size and composition of the work force also influence earnings trends and need to be examined. The figures in Tables 5.2 and 5.3 are based on the work of Levy and Murnane (1992). They illustrate some of the ways in which employment shifts and the changing composition of the work force affect earnings. The first table presents the real annual earnings of groups of year-round, full-time workers over two eight-year periods, 1971–79 and 1979–87. The second documents the number of individuals in each group and their growth rates over the same time periods. Together, these tables show how changes in the demand and supply of different types of labor have resulted in greater earnings inequality.

Worker productivity and earnings reflect individual differences in schooling and on-the-job experience. Analyses of earnings inequality often begin, therefore, with the average wages of different education and age/experience groups. Shifts in the supply and demand for different kinds of labor can be seen in the changing median earnings ratios of the groups. For example, by comparing the average earnings of college and high school graduates, we can measure the payoff from a college education. The top part of Table 5.2 shows that the median wage of college-educated males between the ages of twenty-five and thirty-four was $30,054 in 1971, compared to $24,590 for their high school–educated counterparts. The earnings ratio of the groups was 1.22, as shown in the bottom part of the table. On average, the earnings of young, male college graduates in 1971 were 22 percent higher than those of young, male high school graduates.

Table 5.2.   Earnings of Year-Round, Full-Time Workers (1988 Dollars)

Gender	Age	Years of schooling	Median earnings		
			1971	*1979*	*1987*
Males	All		27,322	27,778	27,898
	25–34	12	24,590	24,537	21,699
		16	30,054	27,778	29,965
	35–54	12	26,896	29,290	27,730
		16	40,984	39,577	39,195
Females	All		15,929	16,204	18,599
	25–34	12	15,082	15,123	15,499
		16	21,311	18,671	22,525
	35–54	12	15,308	15,432	16,406
		16	22,747	20,346	24,112
Ratio of earnings w/16 years schooling to earnings w/12 years schooling					
Males	25–34		1.22	1.13	1.38
	35–54		1.51	1.35	1.42
Females	25–34		1.41	1.23	1.45
	35–54		1.48	1.31	1.47
Ratio of female to male earnings					
			0.58	0.58	0.67

Source: Levy and Murnane (1992, table 5).

Table 5.3.   Group Size in Millions, and Percentage Change in Group Size, of Full-Time Workers

Gender	Age	Years of schooling	Group size 1971	1979	1987	% Change 1971–79	1979–87
Males	All		42.5	47.8	53.3	12	12
	25–34	12	4.15	4.7	6.6	13	40
		16	1.2	2.2	2.9	85	32
	35–54	12	6.0	6.2	7.5	3	21
		16	1.6	2.0	3.4	25	70
Females	All		26.6	36.1	45.2	36	25
	25–34	12	2.4	4.0	5.5	66	37
		16	.7	1.5	2.5	151	67
	35–54	12	4.8	5.9	7.9	23	34
		16	.65	1.2	2.4	85	100

Source: Levy and Murnane (1992, table 6).

This college earnings premium changes over time in the face of supply and demand shifts. The main supply shift during the 1970s was the labor market entry of relatively well-educated baby-boomers. From Table 5.3 we can see that the number of young, college-educated male workers increased by 85 percent between 1971 and 1979 and the number of comparable female workers grew by 151 percent. This huge supply shift exceeded the growth of demand for college-educated workers and led to lower real earnings for both groups. Over the same time period the number of young, high school–educated workers grew more slowly and their real earnings remained fairly constant. As a result, the college earnings premium dropped from 22 to 13 percent among young men and from 41 to 23 percent among young women. Although the number of older, college-educated workers increased less rapidly in the 1970s, their real earnings also declined both absolutely and relative to those of older, high school graduates. The overall effect of the increased supply of college-educated labor was to reduce the college earnings premium for every group.

At the same time that the entry of the baby-boom generation reduced the payoff from a college education, it raised the relative earnings of older cohorts. In economic terms, younger workers are imperfect substitutes for older, more experienced workers with the same level of education. Consequently, as the number of younger workers grew rapidly in the 1970s, the earnings gap between younger and older cohorts widened. The labor market entry of the baby-boomers thus had different effects on the earnings premiums associated with higher education and with work experience, and because of these offsetting effects between-group inequality increased very little over the decade.

The 1980s tell a different story. The number of young, college graduates grew more slowly between 1979 and 1987, and their real earnings increased. The continuing growth in demand for well-educated labor evidently outweighed the increase in its supply. The number of older, college-educated workers grew more rapidly in the 1980s as the baby-boom aged. Yet despite their growing numbers, the real earnings of older, college-educated women rose while those of older, male college graduates fell only slightly. The demand for college-educated workers obviously remained high. In contrast, the real wages of male high school graduates dropped sharply. The median earnings of young, high school–educated males fell from $24,537 to $21,699 between 1979 and 1987, while the earnings of older male high school grads decreased from $29,290 to $27,730. Much of this earnings loss can be traced to changes in the industry composition of employment. The proportion of young, high school–educated men employed in manufacturing went from 38 percent in 1979 to 29 percent in 1987, while the number holding jobs in retail trade increased from 18 to 23 percent. The loss of manufacturing jobs forced a growing percentage of young male high school graduates to seek employment in lower-wage industries. The demand for less-educated workers also declined within industries and especially within manufacturing, where the number of semiskilled jobs decreased more rapidly than overall employment (Katz and Murphy 1992). There has been a sharp decrease in demand for blue-collar workers as a result of both inter- and intraindustry employment shifts, and this demand shift has had a particularly negative impact upon the earnings ability of men without a college education.

The diminished job opportunities of blue-collar workers, combined with the continued growth in demand for college graduates, accounts for much of the rise of earnings inequality during the 1980s. The relative earnings of male and female college graduates of every age improved between 1979 and 1987.[3] The college premium increased among men largely as a result of the real wage losses of less-educated workers. It increased among women because of the real wages gains of those with a college education. For both men and women the increase in the college premium led to greater between-group inequality. The major exception to the trend toward greater inequality can be seen in the relative earnings gains of female workers. The female-male earnings ratio rose from 0.58 in 1979 to 0.67 in 1987. This relative change reflects both the improving employment opportunities of college-educated women and the decreasing earnings ability of less-educated men.

The earnings premiums associated with education and age explain only part of the wage dispersion of the past two decades. Earnings inequality also increased *within* different education and age groups. A major cause of the increased wage dispersion within skill groups was the decline in union density. The proportion of the work force represented by unions fell gradually from the mid-1950s through the 1970s. This trend accelerated in the

1980s, when union representation fell about one percentage point a year. In 1969 about 29 percent of the nonagricultural work force were union members, a proportion that dropped gradually to 25 percent in 1978. By 1989 only 16 percent of the work force and 12 percent of private-sector workers were union members. The fall in union density was even more rapid among male blue-collar workers between the ages of twenty-five and thirty-four. Union membership among this traditionally organized group dropped 18 percentage points during this period (Freeman 1993:137). These declines are not simply a reflection of the shift of employment out of manufacturing: in the 1980s, union density fell in virtually every industry.

Unions have long been criticized for increasing the wages of organized workers relative to those of nonunion members. What is seldom appreciated is the extent to which unions reduce wage inequality. Unions reduce the variability of wages among union members both within and across establishments, and they raise the wages of blue-collar workers relative to those of white-collar workers. Union wage policies reduce earnings inequality within establishments by attaching wages to jobs rather than to individuals. These single-rate pay schemes foster worker solidarity and reduce the effect of arbitrary decisions and favoritism in wage setting. Unions also attempt to equalize the pay of workers in similar jobs across establishments so that wages and wage cutting do not enter into interfirm competition. Major collective bargaining agreements reveal the importance attached to standardizing wages across establishments. Finally, unionization narrows the wage gap between white-collar and blue-collar workers. The overall effect of union representation is a substantial reduction in wage inequality.[4]

Because of these inequality-reducing effects, the decline in union density has contributed to earnings differences within skill groups. In a recent study Richard Freeman (1993:159) estimates that the fall in union density accounted for 20 percent of the overall increase in male earnings inequality between 1978 and 1988. He cautiously concludes that "declining unionization was a supporting player in the story of the increase in inequality—not the main character: Rosencrantz or Guildenstern, not Hamlet." Not Hamlet, surely, but maybe Horatio. The shift of employment away from heavily unionized sectors and the drop in union membership within industries have resulted in greater wage dispersion within education and age groups.

FAMILY INCOME AND POVERTY TRENDS

What happens to individuals in the labor market directly affects families. Wages and salaries are the main source of income for all but a very small percentage of the population, and the median family income closely follows earnings trends. The correspondence between individual earnings and family income is not perfect, however. More and more families rely upon multiple wage earners to maintain their income position; they have been able to raise their real incomes by sending more family members into the work force. The median family income (in 1992 dollars) went from $35,821 in 1973 to $38,710 in 1989, before falling to $36,812 in 1992. Over the same period the proportion of families with multiple earners increased from 53.9 to over 58 percent (Devine and Wright 1993:37).

Most of the increased labor force participation is among married women with children under the age of six. Today, three-fifths of married women with young children are in the paid work force, compared to about one-third of such women in 1973. Without this increased participation the median family income would be below its 1973 level. And despite this increased labor force involvement, there has probably been a net loss in the economic welfare of the average family. Higher day care and transportation expenses substantially reduce the earnings gains of many families when both parents work. The ability of families to compensate for lower individual earnings through increased labor force activity may also be reaching its limits. As the labor force participation rate of married women levels off, median family income should track earnings trends even more closely.

Wages and salaries are the main source of income for most families, but they do not represent the main income source of the very poor and the very rich. Those at the bottom end of the income distribution depend upon government income supports and in-kind benefits, and real social spending on the poor decreased during the 1980s. Those at the top end of the income distribution receive much of their income from assets, and investment income grew rapidly during the 1980s. These divergent trends in transfer payments and property income, in addition to the increased dispersion in worker earnings, have resulted in greater family income inequality.

The summary measure of income inequality used by the Census Bureau is the Gini index. This index varies from 0 to 1.0 and can be interpreted as the proportion of the total income that would have to be redistributed for all income shares to be equal. Used to measure family income, the index rose from a postwar low of .348 in 1968 to a postwar high of .401 in 1989 (Devine and Wright 1993:32).[5] A more detailed picture of the changes in family income inequality can be seen in the income distributions presented in Table 5.4. Throughout the postwar period the richest fifth of all families received over 40 percent of the total income and the poorest fifth got about 5 percent, although prior to 1973 there was a modest trend toward a more equal distribution. Since then, the income distribution has become increasingly skewed as approximately 3 percent of the total income was redistributed from the bottom three-fifths of the population to the top fifth. This regressive redistribution may appear modest, but it had a disproportionate effect upon the poorest families. The income share of the bottom fifth has

Table 5.4.   Distribution of Before-Tax Family Income

	Change (%)			
	1947	*1973*	*1992*	*1973–92*
Poorest fifth	5.0	5.5	4.4	−20.0
Second fifth	11.8	11.9	10.5	−11.8
Middle fifth	17.0	17.5	16.5	−5.7
Fourth fifth	23.1	24.0	24.0	0.0
Richest fifth	43.0	41.1	44.6	8.5

Source: *Statistical Abstract of the United States,* various years.

decreased by 20 percent, and that of the next poorest fifth by nearly 12 percent. Again, it is important to realize that as long as the median income grows very slowly, this inegalitarian trend represents a net loss of social welfare. An extra thousand dollars means little to a family making seventy-five thousand dollars a year, but it makes a great deal of difference to one with an annual income of ten thousand dollars. The richest fifth of families may not have noticed any major changes in their standard of living, but the poorest fifth have certainly experienced a marked decline in theirs.

As the income gap separating American families has widened, the population of poor has grown. The official poverty threshold was introduced in 1964 in conjunction with the Johnson administration's War on Poverty and has been used to estimate the number of poor for every year from 1959 to the present. Based upon the cost of an "emergency temporary low-budget diet," this poverty baseline represents an absolute standard that does not increase in real terms. Up until the mid-1970s, both the number and the percentage of families with incomes below the poverty line decreased. This egalitarian trend reversed during the 1970s, and the poor have since grown both in absolute number and as a percentage of the population. Comparing across the business cycle peaks of 1979 and 1989, the number of families living in poverty increased from 5.3 to 6.8 million, or from 9.1 to 10.3 percent of all families (U.S. Bureau of the Census 1994:479).

A common explanation for the rise in poverty points to the changes in family structure, and particularly to the growing number of female-headed households. These single-parent families are more likely to depend upon government assistance for their support, and their numbers increased rapidly in the 1960s and 1970s. But much of the rise in poverty during the 1980s was among two-parent families, and most of the increase was accounted for by working families. In 1990 almost three-fifths of all poverty households had at least one household member who was employed and nearly one-fifth had more than one (Devine and Wright 1993:50). The problem is not that these families are unwilling to work: it is that they are unable to work long enough at jobs that pay enough to keep them above the poverty line. One reason for the lower real earnings of these families was the reduced buying power of the federal minimum wage. Approximately two million people work full-time at a minimum wage standard that has lost much of its buying power in recent years. Only part of this lost buying power was restored when Congress finally raised the minimum wage in 1990, and the value of the minimum wage has of course decreased since then.

The growing number of poor is a consequence of slower growth and heightened earnings inequality. The labor market offers fewer opportunities to inexperienced or less-educated workers, and the longest economic expansion in postwar history did not prevent millions of additional people from falling below the poverty line. The recent recession and the low rate of job creation since 1989 added many more people to the poverty rolls, but improvement in the macroeconomy alone will not reverse the poverty trend. A key lesson of the 1980s is that business expansions are no longer raising the earnings ability of low-income workers or preventing the growth of poverty among American families.

ARE WE IN SEPARATE BOATS?

In his influential book *The Work of Nations*, Secretary of Labor Robert Reich (1991) argues that the domestic economy is ceasing to exist as a system of production and exchange separate from the rest of the world. Reich envisions a global economy in which national corporations are evolving into global enterprise webs. As heightened competition and a changing consumer demand reduce the profit margins on standardized goods, the high-value production of new or customized products and the ability to link those products to the unique needs of particular customers become the source of most profits. Consequently, the corporation is being transformed into an "array of decentralized groups and subgroups continuously contracting" for the skills and insights involved in this high-value production wherever those skills and insights can be found.

The earnings ability of a nation's workers and the living standards of its families have thus come to depend upon the position they occupy within the emerging global economy or, more precisely, upon the value that their skills add to global enterprise webs. The vast majority of workers fall into the three functional categories of routine production services, in-person services, and symbolic-analytic services.[6] Depending upon which of these functions we perform, our economic fortunes are rapidly diverging. To use Reich's (1991:208) metaphor, we occupy "different boats, one sinking rapidly, one sinking more slowly, and the third rising steadily."

In this descriptive scenario, the boat occupied by routine producers is sinking rapidly. As the costs of transporting materials and goods decrease and as the speed of communicating large amounts of information becomes instantaneous, high-volume production and data-processing operations can be located at low-cost sites around the world. Routine producers in this country must now compete against workers in newly industrialized countries with wage levels far below ours. This competition exerts tremendous downward pressure upon employment and wages and explains the collapse of demand for blue-collar labor. Routine production services are closely identified with manufacturing, but they also include many jobs in finance, insurance, and other service industries. Information-processing tasks can now be carried out in Irish villages or on Caribbean islands and then transmitted instantly via satellite to corporate headquarters in different parts of the world.

In-person servers also perform routine functions. They include waiters and waitresses, cabdrivers, janitors, domestic help, security guards, and retail sales workers. These jobs typically involve physical contact or the proximity of server and client and therefore cannot be exported. But many in-person services can be provided by undocumented workers who are willing to work for low wages, and the jobs themselves are often replaced by labor-saving technologies such as automated tellers, computerized information processing, and robotic devices. In our global economy, the boat occupied by personal servers is sinking slowly.

Symbolic analysts provide the problem-solving, problem-identifying, and brokering skills that are the basis of high-value production. Their numbers include many lawyers, bankers, real estate developers, engineers, scientists, writers, performers, and any others whose skills are crucial to the manipulation of information, financial assets, and people. The skills of some symbolic analysts are in much greater demand than those of others, and the rewards that they reap are correspondingly larger. Nonetheless, these highly trained and skilled workers are all linked to a global economy in which the demand for their services continues to grow. Their boat is steadily rising.

The shift to high-value production and the transformation of national corporations into global enterprise webs affect more than worker earnings. Reich sees these changes undermining the ties of economic interdependence that binds us together as a nation. The growing demand for the skills of symbolic analysts within an international labor market means that their financial well-being no longer depends upon the productivity or purchasing power of their fellow citizens. At a time when the nation becomes increasingly dependent upon the fortunate fifth who sell their services on a world market, they become less dependent upon the rest of the nation. Their position within the global labor market separates them from the majority of Americans and threatens to undermine any shared sense of national purpose. The informal norms that have restrained wage inequality in the past gradually lose their force. As inequality increases, there is a danger that the more fortunate fifth of the population will gradually secede from the larger society and retreat into private enclaves.

Evidence of the weakening ties of economic interdependence can be seen in the unprecedented growth of executive compensation. The transformation of corporations into global webs means that their stakeholders have become a very large and dispersed group. The organizational linkages and sense of common purpose that connected management and production workers are being broken, and so is the implicit social contract that once restrained the growth of executive salaries. In 1960 the chief executives of the one hundred largest U.S. corporations reported average earnings of $190,000, about forty times the wage of the typical factory worker. By 1988, the executive officers of the largest corporations received, on average, over $2 million, more than ninety-three times the wage of the typical production worker. The difference in take-home pay has increased even more rapidly than these salary figures because the maximum tax rate was much higher in 1960 than in 1988. The after-tax income of these chief executives went from twelve times that of production workers to more than seventy times as much (Reich 1991:204–5).

Reich (1991:205) acknowledges in a footnote that the level of executive compensation is much higher in this country than in Europe and Japan. A 1990 survey found that the total compensation of the chief executive officers of large U.S. corporations was 50 percent higher than that of their Japanese counterparts and 90 percent higher than the compensation of German and British CEOs. What is not explained is how these differences in executive compensation persist in the face of global enterprise webs and the weakening economic ties within nations. After all, the centrifugal forces of the global economy also operate upon the informal norms that restrain executive salaries in Europe and Japan. It is not clear why the emerging global economy should have a more pronounced effect upon the compensation of U.S. executives.

Metaphors often make complex realities more comprehensible, but they also simplify and sometimes distort those realities. The imagery of separate boats dramatizes the unequal impact of a more open world economy upon the earnings ability of people in different jobs. It recalls and implicitly contrasts with Kennedy's oft-cited statement that the rising tide of economic growth lifts all boats. Although Reich's imagery is compelling, it disregards the institutional determinants of earnings and conveys only part of the threat to American living standards. First of all, the reported demise of the national economy is greatly exaggerated. Global enterprise webs radiate from a home country, and their actions are regulated or influenced to varying degrees by the laws and institutions of those countries. Because of our tax and tariff codes, U.S. firms have been much more inclined than their Japanese and European counterparts to move production operations offshore in search of lower-cost labor (Grunwald and Flamm 1985). The effects of a changing labor demand are also mediated by wage-setting institutions that regulate national labor markets and help to maintain worker earnings. Most European countries enforce a higher minimum wage than the United States, and most offer employees some form of collective representation, either through a union or through the works councils that operate within establishments. The level of unionization fell in several other industrial countries over the past decade, but the decline in the United States was exceptional.

These institutional differences help to explain why earnings inequality increased sharply in this country during the 1980s, while it increased only slightly or not at all in Japan and most European countries. They also explain why the United States is the only advanced country in which the real earnings of lower-paid workers declined. According to a report by the National Bureau of Economic Research, the real earnings of American men in the lowest decile of the earnings distribution decreased between 11 and 17 percent (depending upon the wage survey used) over the past decade. By 1992 their earnings averaged just 38 percent of the U.S. median wage. By comparison, men in the bottom decile averaged 61 percent of the median wage in Japan and 68 percent in Europe. Despite our high overall standard of living, the working poor are worse off in both absolute and relative terms in the United States than in any other major industrial country. At the same time, men at the top of the earnings distribution, and not just corporate executives, do relatively better. American men in the top decile receive 2.14 times the median wage, while the comparable ratio is 1.73 in Japan and 1.78 in West Europe (Freeman 1994:12–13). The causes of this comparatively greater earnings inequality are to be found within American society—they are not the inevitable result of an increasingly global economy.

A nation's living standards ultimately depend upon the skills of its work force, as Reich emphasizes. However, those skills remain interdependent. If production and nonsupervisory workers cannot master new technologies, the so-called symbolic analysts will also become less productive. The skills of those who make up the bottom two-thirds of the earnings distribution are the foundation that supports the productivity and earnings ability of the entire work force. There will always be prominent examples of highly talented or well-connected professionals and executives who benefit from global economic networks while the earnings of their countrymen stagnate or decline. Andrew Lloyd Webber's musicals have made him fabulously wealthy because they play to a global audience, but the earnings ability of the vast majority of talented British professionals and managers is comparatively low because the productivity of the British work force remains comparatively low. The increased earnings inequality in this country may indicate that we are in separate boats, but the slowdown in productivity and earnings growth reminds us that the boats are tied together. If two of the boats sink far enough, they will eventually drag the third one down as well.

NOTES

1. As discussed in Chapter 2, the persistence of industry wage differentials that cannot be explained in terms of worker or job characteristics represents a theoretical anomaly (Thaler, 1989).

2. Costrell's findings are reported in Mishel (1989).

3. The real earnings of college graduates fell 1.6 percent during the three-year period beginning in 1989, a decline that eliminated much of their wage gains over the preceding decade (Uchitelle 1992).

4. Estimates of the inequality-reducing effects of unions are presented in Freeman and Medoff (1984:89–93).

5. The Gini index fell slightly in 1990 to .396.

6. These functional categories of labor are described in Reich (1991:208–24).

Worker Displacement and
Contemporary Unemployment 6

> Perhaps the most plausible explanation for what has been called "transitional unemployment" is that workers who have lost high-wage jobs find it difficult to accept their fate and so prefer remaining unemployed to acknowledging the permanence of their job loss by taking a low-wage job.
>
> —Lawrence Summers, *Understanding Unemployment*

Between 1970 and 1989, the U.S. civilian labor force added more than thirty-eight million employees. The economy employed an increasing percentage of the adult population during a period in which that population expanded very rapidly, and it did so without running persistently high levels of unemployment. The rate of employment growth slowed in the late 1980s, and it came to a halt between 1989 and 1992 as the economy went into recession. Still, judging from the record of employment growth over the past two decades, the U.S. economy has performed comparatively well.

This record of job creation notwithstanding, the trend rate of unemployment rose to a level well above its postwar average: from 1948 to 1973 unemployment averaged 4.8 percent; from 1973 to 1993 it averaged 7.0 percent. An important clue to the sources of this trend increase can be found in the changing composition of the unemployed population. Unemployment rose among all demographic groups during the 1970s and 1980s, but the increase was greatest among males of prime working age. A group traditionally characterized by its strong labor force attachment and employment stability now accounts for a growing portion of total unemployment. The labor market situation of these prime-age workers has worsened.

Chapter 3 discussed the obstacles to reemployment that displaced workers face. This chapter resumes that discussion by looking at the relationship between job loss and the higher average unemployment rate of the past two decades. The upward trend in unemployment is often attributed to higher wage expectations, particularly among lower-wage workers, and to the increased turnover associated with changes in the demographic composition of the labor force. The logic underlying these explanations is summarized below, along with the evidence that suggests that rising wage expectations and normal labor force turnover do not adequately explain higher unemployment. An alternative interpretation presented here highlights the increased rates of job loss and the lengthening unemployment spells among men of prime working age. It traces the trend increase in unemployment to the displacement of workers who have traditionally been their families' primary wage support. Their inability to find jobs comparable in pay to those they have lost has resulted in longer unemployment spells.

THE SOCIAL WAGE AND SEARCH UNEMPLOYMENT

Before the depression of the 1930s, unemployment was usually explained in terms of the qualifications and wage demands of the unemployed. Economic doctrine held that labor was like any other commodity, its supply and demand regulated by a market wage, so the presence of unemployment simply meant that wages were too high. In a properly functioning market, this imbalance should be self-correcting. That is, the presence of individuals anxious to find work should cause wages to fall. The characterization of most unemployment as voluntary derives from this neoclassical perspective. As long as job-seekers are free to reduce their wage demands, the length of unemployment spells appears to be a matter of individual preference and choice.

This conventional explanation lost credibility in the face of the hardships of the depression, when real wages fell dramatically yet millions were unable to find work. The publication of John Maynard Keynes's *General Theory of Employment, Interest and Money* in the mid-1930s cast the problem of unemployment in a new light. Keynes argued that the expectations of private investors, not the wage demands of individual workers, were the cause of mass unemployment.[1] When business expectations regarding the future growth of the economy are severely depressed, investors will not invest and the level of economic demand will remain too low to provide jobs for all the people seeking work. Under these conditions, cutting wages will only reduce consumer demand and depress business expectations further. Lowering wages will not solve the problem of insufficient demand or eliminate unemployment. Only an active macroeconomic policy that sustains both consumer buying power and investor confidence will assure sufficient demand to create new job opportunities. From this Keynesian perspective, unemployment is a social as well as an individual problem, and a public policy issue of foremost importance.

During the quarter-century following the Second World War, Keynes's analysis of the macroeconomy won widespread acceptance and provided the economic rationale for new social welfare and income transfer programs. These programs not only bolstered the purchasing power of hard-pressed families; they also raised the level of consumer demand and contributed to the continued growth of the economy. Conservative critics objected to this increased social spending on the grounds that it raised wage expectations. From their perspective, social spending programs represent a growing public contribution to what is often termed the social wage, the combination of transfer payments and market wages that together determine living standards. As long as economic growth continued and unemployment remained low, this conservative viewpoint garnered little public support. But as unemployment rose during the 1970s and appeared increasingly unresponsive to macroeconomic policy, both income maintenance programs and the Keynesian analysis of unemployment came under fire.

Government transfer programs were blamed for raising wage demands and for weakening the work force commitment of the unemployed. They were portrayed as the cause of unemployment, rather than the solution. The explanation for widespread unemployment had thus come full circle. Unemployment was again thought to be the result of a wage, albeit a social one, above the market-clearing level, but the solution to this unemployment problem was no longer simply a matter of individual choice. Because wage levels have a public as well as a private component, the proposed solution calls for reducing or eliminating social spending programs.

The neoclassical perspective with its characteristic emphasis upon wage expectations reemerged in the 1970s in the guise of job search theory. As previously discussed, job search theory emphasizes how expectations in the form of the reservation wage balance the costs of continued search against the benefit of obtaining a better job offer. Income transfers and social programs maintain the reservation wage by reducing the income loss due to unemployment. Unemployment benefits in particular subsidize longer average periods of search and result in better eventual job matches. Of course, the longer the expected period of search, the greater the number of people unemployed at any point in time and the higher the unemployment rate.

As an explanation for the higher average unemployment of the past two decades, this logic can be criticized on the grounds of timing. Simply put, the public components of the social wage have not increased over the past two decades. The real benefit levels of unemployment compensation, the major source of income support for the unemployed, have not risen since the 1960s. In addition, the percentage of unemployed workers who receive compensation has fallen dramatically because program eligibility is increasingly restricted (Council of Economic Advisors 1988:80). Other social welfare programs are likely to affect the wage expectations of low-wage workers. These programs grew rapidly during the 1960s when unemployment was low, but since then the real income support for the poor has declined. It is difficult to see how the public contribution to the social wage could account for the increasing duration of unemployment spells during a period in which income transfers to the unemployed and to the poor decreased.

NORMAL TURNOVER AND THE
INFLATION-UNEMPLOYMENT TRADE-OFF

A related explanation for higher average unemployment stresses the changing composition of the work force. As unemployment trended upward in the 1970s, a number of analysts argued that demographic changes in the work force were leading to increased turnover.[2] They portrayed a labor market in which the flow of people into and out of unemployment was quite large, and in which unemployment spells were frequent and brief. They attributed this instability to the labor force entry of so-called secondary workers, primarily married women and teenagers. By definition, secondary workers are not their families' main wage support, and their attachment to the work force is weaker than that of primary wage-earners. They are more likely to quit, to move from one job to another, and to exit and then reenter the labor force as employment conditions change.

Any dynamic economy generates some frictional unemployment as a result of labor turnover, the rate at which people are hired, laid off, or quit. Even when job opportunities are widely available, it takes time for people to find suitable employment. In addition, there are group differences in the frequency with which people change jobs, in the length of time they spend looking for work, and in the likelihood that they will withdraw from or reenter the work force. When the composition of the labor force changes, these group differences in the turnover rate can affect the level of unemployment. The rapid labor force entry of inexperienced or secondary workers during the 1970s was thought to have resulted in higher unemployment because of this increased turnover.

This explanation appears less compelling than it once did. If the demographic shift toward a younger and increasingly female work force contributed to higher unemployment during the 1970s, it was at least partly offset by the improved educational level of work force entrants (see Table 5.3). The baby-boom generation was better educated than previous cohorts, and job turnover is lower among college-educated workers. More importantly, the trend toward a younger and less experienced labor force reversed long ago. By 1980 the average age and experience level of the work force had begun to rise, thereby contributing to greater employment stability. Yet unemployment remained fairly high throughout most of the past decade.

The following section shows that the demographic characteristics of the unemployed population are not consistent with turnover explanations of higher unemployment. Before discussing the changing demographics of the unemployed, it is important to understand why turnover models have been so influential. One reason for their popularity may be that they portray unemployment in a way that minimizes its costs and deprivations. After all, unemployment figures measure the proportion of the work force that is actively seeking work, but they do not directly measure economic hardship. They do not show the percentage of the population that is employed, or whether the unemployed are the primary wage earners, or whether they come from families where there are other wage earners. If most unemployment spells are brief and are concentrated among secondary workers, as turnover models suggest, then the hardships of unemployment are widely shared and do not represent a major threat to family well-being. Some groups may exhibit a great deal of instability, moving from one job to another, but most unemployment is due to the turnover that is normal for a dynamic economy and a rapidly changing work force. The most effective way to reduce unemployment, therefore, is through measures that facilitate job search or create stronger job attachment. Efforts to expand employment are not necessary and may be counterproductive. To the extent that unemployment is the product of voluntary turnover, (Keynesian) policies that stimulate the economy and raise the level of employment will only prove inflationary.

Turnover models of unemployment thus provide the basic rationale for the anti-inflation policies of the Federal Reserve Board. Given that some labor market turnover is necessary and inevitable, economists assume that there is a "natural" rate of unemployment that is consistent with stable inflation. This unemployment level is termed the "nonaccelerating inflation rate of unemployment," or NAIRU.[3] If we reduce unemployment below this long-term trend, labor markets will tighten, workers will be able to demand wage increases that exceed productivity growth, and firms will raise prices in excess of costs. To arrest this inflationary spiral, the demand for labor must then fall until unemployment rises above the NAIRU. In short, there is a trade-off between unemployment and inflation. Since any attempt to reduce unemployment below the level of normal turnover will lead to higher inflation, this trade-off represents a major obstacle to lower unemployment.

The Federal Reserve Board can influence the demand for labor and reduce unemployment by lowering interest rates, but it usually acts with extreme caution for fear of igniting inflation. Nobody knows exactly what the NAIRU is at any given moment. But if normal job turnover has increased because of the changing composition of the work force, then the trade-off between unemployment and inflation has worsened, and higher levels of unemployment are necessary to control inflation. The belief that the NAIRU has risen thus argues against taking measures to combat unemployment. Rather, it calls for a tighter monetary policy on the part of the Federal Reserve.

It seems surprising given the importance of the inflation-unemployment trade-off for macroeconomic policy, but there appears to be little relationship between inflation and unemployment in recent years. During the 1950s and 1960s the terms of the trade-off were comparatively stable; unemployment rates were low in the years that inflation was high. This stable relationship ended in the 1970s when both unemployment and inflation rose. It appeared then that ever higher levels of unemployment were necessary to restrain inflation. Yet if the terms of the trade-off worsened in the 1970s, they must have improved in the 1980s. When unemployment fell during the latter part of the past decade, inflation remained at roughly 4 percent.[4] The drop in unemployment did not lead to higher inflation. Nor is there any evidence that lower rates of unemployment are having much effect upon inflation during the current business upturn that began in 1992. Clearly, the terms of the trade-off between unemployment and inflation change for reasons that are not well understood.

The belief in a NAIRU rests upon the indisputable fact that some labor force turnover is necessary and normal. Consequently, there is going to be a trade-off between unemployment and inflation at some point. That does not mean that lower unemployment leads to higher inflation, or vice versa. Inflation and unemployment can move independently over very wide ranges. Rather than assuming that efforts to reduce unemployment will prove inflationary, we need to find ways to lower the NAIRU—the point at which unemployment does become inflationary. The goal should be to eliminate, insofar as is possible, the trade-off between unemployment and inflation.

JOB LOSS AND LONGER UNEMPLOYMENT SPELLS

In a series of widely cited studies, Lawrence Summers and his colleagues disputed the empirical claims of turnover explanations of unemployment.[5] They argued that normal turnover accounts for a relatively small and constant portion of the higher average unemployment of the past two decades. Although most spells are brief, as turnover models suggest, unemployment is concentrated in lengthy spells, and it is these longer spells that account for the trend increase in unemployment.

The significance of this finding is best illustrated with an example. Imagine that each week ten out of every thousand workers begin an unemployment spell that lasts for one week. On any given week the unemployment rate would be 1 percent. Now imagine that each week one additional person enters unemployment and remains unemployed for ten weeks. The · average length of the unemployment spells will be only 1.8 weeks, indicating that most unemployment spells are brief, but half of all unemployment is now concentrated in the longer spell. As long as the pattern recurs, there will be twenty people unemployed each week, and the unemployment rate will have doubled to 2 percent. At any given time, half of the unemployed will be in the midst of the longer ten-week spells, and they will account for half of the unemployment rate. Unemployment is thus concentrated in lengthy spells, and any change in the number of such spells has a disproportionate impact upon the total amount of unemployment and the unemployment rate.

The importance of long jobless spells would be more apparent were it not for the way that unemployment is defined. To be classified as unemployed, an individual must be "actively looking for work." This definition is ambiguous, and the distinction between being unemployed and being out of the work force is not very meaningful for those who have become too discouraged to actively look for work. A substantial portion of unemployment is classified as labor force withdrawal. In fact, the movement of individuals into and out of the work force dominates all other labor market flows, yet as many as half of those who withdraw from the labor force say that they want "a regular job now." Because of the somewhat artificial distinction between unemployment and labor force withdrawal, the average length of unemployment spells understates the actual length of time it takes most people to move between jobs. Even during the highly favorable labor market conditions of 1969, less than half of those who became unemployed found jobs within three months when periods of labor force withdrawal are taken into account (Summers 1990:12–15). The belief that most unemployment consists of short transitions between jobs is wrong. Unemployment is concentrated in long spells, and the official unemployment figures underestimate the duration of those spells.

This measurement bias notwithstanding, the average length of unemployment spells has clearly increased. The first column of Table 6.1 reports the percentage of all unemployment spells that lasted six months or more during the peaks and troughs of recent business cycles. Comparing peak and trough years reveals that most of the cyclical variation in the unemployment rate is due to the changing incidence of long spells. The percentage of prolonged

Table 6.1.   The Long-Term Unemployed, 1969–92

	Year	Spells of 6 months or more	Unemployment rates		Percentage due to Job loss
			Total	Job loss	
Peak	1969	4.7	3.5	1.3	37.1
	1973	7.9	4.9	1.9	38.8
	1979	8.7	5.8	2.5	43.1
	1989	9.9	5.3	2.4	45.3
Trough	1971	10.3	5.9	2.7	45.8
	1975	15.2	8.5	4.7	55.3
	1982	16.6	9.7	5.7	58.8
	1992	20.6	7.4	4.2	56.8

Source: *Employment and Earnings,* various issues.

Table 6.2. Unemployment Rates By Age-Sex and Marital Status, 1969–92

Age-sex	Peaks		Change (%)	Troughs		Change (%)
	1969	1989	1969–89	1971	1992	1971–92
All men	2.8	5.2	86	5.3	7.8	47
16–19	11.4	15.9	39	16.6	21.5	30
20–24	5.1	8.8	73	10.3	12.2	18
25–54	1.6	4.1	156	3.5	6.6	89
55–64	1.8	3.5	94	3.3	5.8	76
All women	4.7	5.4	15	6.9	6.9	0
16–19	13.3	14.0	5	17.2	18.5	8
20–24	6.3	8.3	32	9.6	10.2	6
25–54	3.5	4.4	26	5.3	6.0	13
55–64	2.2	2.8	27	3.3	4.2	27
Married men	1.7	3.0	43	3.7	5.0	35
Married women	3.7	3.7	0	5.9	5.0	−15

Sources: U.S. Department of Labor (1989, tables 28 and 55); Employment and Earnings, various issues.

unemployment spells during recession years is roughly double what it is at the peak of the business cycle. Controlling for this cyclical variation, the incidence of long-term unemployment has increased steadily for more than twenty years. Looking at the peak years, the number of long-term spells increased from 4.7 percent of the total in 1969 to 9.9 percent in 1989. Comparing the recession years, the proportion of long-term spells increased from 10.3 percent in 1971 to 20.6 percent in 1992. During the period as a whole, the incidence of lengthy unemployment spells more than doubled.

This increase in the number of long spells is associated with higher rates of job loss. The other columns of Table 6.1 present the overall unemployment rate, the unemployment rate due to job loss, and their ratio—the percentage of total unemployment due to job loss. Because many job losers withdraw from the labor force and are then classified as reentrants when they resume active search, these figures underreport the amount of unemployment due to job loss. They show a clear trend, nonetheless. At the peak of the business cycle, the job loss component rose from 37.1 percent of unemployment in 1969 to 45.3 percent in 1989. At the troughs it went from 45.8 percent in 1971 to 58.8 percent in 1982, dropping slightly to 56.8 percent in 1992. Another way to demonstrate the significance of the job loss rate is to subtract it from the total unemployment rate. Stripped of its job loss component, unemployment shows little trend, moving between 2.3 and 3.3 percent at business cycle peaks and between 3.2 and 4.0 during recessions. Most of the trend increase over the past two decades is explained by the increasing incidence of the prolonged unemployment spells that follow job loss.

The increase in job loss and in the incidence of lengthy unemployment spells appears to be concentrated among males of prime working age. Table 6.2 presents a breakdown by age and gender of the unemployment rates, and the percentage change in those rates, for the peak employment years of 1969 and 1989 and the recession years of 1971 and 1992. While the female unemployment rate shows little change, the male rate almost doubled between 1969 and 1989 and increased by nearly half between 1971 and 1992. This increase in male unemployment is greatest among those twenty-five to fifty-four years of age. The unemployment rate of men in this age group rose 156 percent between the two peak employment years and 89 percent between the two recession years. The sharp increase in unemployment among prime-age males also contrasts with the high but comparatively stable rates among teenagers, both male and female. Although it is not evident from the table, teenagers represented a declining percentage of the work force throughout this period, and their share of total unemployment dropped sharply.[6]

The same pattern emerges when we compare the unemployment rates of married men and married women. Married men traditionally have the most stable employment histories of any group, yet their unemployment rate has risen substantially and appears to have converged with that of married women. The higher average unemployment of recent years thus cannot be attributed to normal job turnover among teenagers and female workers. Unemployment is increasingly concentrated among married men of prime working age, and this change is primarily the result of higher rates of job loss and longer unemployment spells. These men are not typically secondary workers. Their unemployment clearly threatens the economic security and welfare of families.

FROM STRUCTURAL TO TRANSITIONAL UNEMPLOYMENT

Few aspects of conventional labor market analysis meet with greater skepticism than the claim that most unemployment is voluntary. Depression-era photos of ruined and desperate people, or more contemporary images of thousands of jobless waiting for hours to apply for a few advertised positions, would seem to contradict and discredit the idea that people choose to be without work. Still, there is an element of choice in all human behavior, and viewing actions as voluntary highlights that element. The view that unemployment is voluntary is consistent with a theory that assumes people have stable, consistent preferences and that their behavior can be explained in terms of rational choices based upon those preferences. Strictly speaking, almost everyone could find some sort of job, if only through self-employment, as long as they are willing to accept very low earnings. Viewing unemployment as voluntary simply means that the unemployed could choose to work at a very low wage if necessary.

In criticizing the notion of voluntary unemployment, we should not deny that there is a significant element of choice in employment decisions. A better approach is to show how choice is exercised within a social context and how the notion of voluntary unemployment violates the cultural standards that define reasonable or acceptable alternatives. Unemployment is involuntary when no available job offers reasonable compensation. Of course, this approach requires that we define what is meant by reasonable. In judging the acceptability of job offers, people compare their present situation to what they have known as well as to the earnings of those with similar qualifications and experience. We may regard a person as involuntarily unemployed, then, if he or she is unable to find a job offering wages comparable to those received by workers of similar ability and training and chooses to wait for an acceptable offer.

Critics of the notion of voluntary unemployment often argue that much unemployment is structural in nature. Structural unemployment denotes a persistent imbalance between the supply and the demand for certain skills within local labor markets. The problem is not one of insufficient demand within the national economy because unfilled jobs and labor scarcities can exist alongside widespread unemployment. Rather, the problem is the mismatch between the skills of the unemployed and the requirements of available jobs. Structural explanations of unemployment gained currency in the late 1950s and early 1960s when automation was thought to be creating skill mismatches in many sectors of the economy (Killingsworth 1966). Most federal employment and training programs were inaugurated during this period, largely in response to this perceived threat. Today, this explanation seems less compelling. Although the unemployment spells of many job losers begin with the collapse of local demand for their skills and experience, the increasing duration of unemployment is not easily explained in terms of skill mismatches. There is more than the obsolescence of job skills behind the rising incidence of long-term unemployment among primary wage earners.

For workers in small and isolated markets where there are no comparable employment opportunities or for those who have invested a large part of their working lives acquiring highly specific skills, a job loss can have an extremely negative and long-term effect upon earnings. But skill obsolescence offers a less-compelling explanation for the prolonged unemployment of experienced workers within large urban labor markets. Experienced and motivated workers who lack specific skills should still be of considerable value to many employers. Under competitive conditions, those displaced from one firm should be able to find jobs by working for somewhat less than the prevailing wage at other firms. To state the issue a little differently, employers should respond to a surplus of experienced workers by cutting wages and expanding employment, but they do not. This absence of competitive wage setting, and the unemployment that results, cannot be attributed to mismatched skills.

Perhaps the clearest indicator of the failure of wages to adjust to the supply of qualified workers is the persistence of large wage gaps between comparable workers doing comparable jobs in different industries. This interindustry wage differential is usually blamed upon institutional barriers to competitive wage setting, such as unions and government regulation. Yet industry differences exist even where there are few institutional constraints on wage cutting, and unions in particular have been shown to account for only a small part of the industry wage pattern (Dickens and Katz 1987). A more convincing explanation for the absence of wage cutting points to the profit-maximizing strategies of firms. Large firms with some degree of market power may find it profitable to pay above-market wages, that is, wages that are higher than needed to assure an adequate supply of labor. As was previously discussed, offering a premium wage improves morale, reduces turnover and hiring costs, and encourages greater worker effort. Paying above-market wages better enables employers to motivate, train, and retain employees, and thereby helps to ensure a more productive work force. In return for cooperation and higher levels of effort on the part of their employees, employers may willingly forgo opportunities to hire workers at lower wage rates.

The fact that it is efficient for some employers to pay more than the market-clearing wage explains why the number of qualified workers exceeds the number of high-wage jobs, but it does not explain why displaced workers would remain unemployed while waiting for another well-paying job to become available. The income support provided by unemployment insurance subsidizes job search and prolongs unemployment spells: it might account for this wait unemployment. The problem with this explanation has already been mentioned. The real benefit levels of unemployment compensation have not increased, and the percentage of the unemployed who receive benefits has dropped sharply over the past twenty years.

To explain the longer jobless spells of experienced workers, we need to view employment and hiring decisions within their social context. People who lose high-wage jobs do not want to regard their situation as permanent. They may prefer remaining unemployed to accepting a low-wage job that confirms a loss of status, in their own eyes and in the eyes of others. In addition, many employers are hesitant to hire workers accustomed to higher wages. They assume that these workers are simply waiting for a better job to become available. As a result, those displaced from well-paying jobs often enter a period of transitional or wait unemployment. Their unemployment is involuntary in the sense that they cannot find a job offering wages comparable to what they formerly earned, but they are hesitant to accept, and may not immediately be offered, jobs that entail a substantial loss of income and status.

The high average unemployment of recent years is largely transitional in nature. It is concentrated among primary workers who have been displaced and who are likely to remain out of work for long periods. Very little of the increase in unemployment can be attributed to secondary workers whose weak labor force attachment leads to high rates of turnover. The shift of employment from high- to low-wage industries and the elimination of well-paying jobs within industries may or may not create a mismatch between the skills of those displaced and the requirements of available jobs. It definitely creates a mismatch between the living standards of many displaced workers and the earnings opportunities available to them. Many cannot find jobs with wages comparable to what they once received or to what similarly qualified workers still receive. Anxious to hold on to a way of life, they enter into what are often prolonged periods of transitional unemployment with all the negative consequences that this entails.

The variation in unemployment rates across states and regions supports this interpretation. Summers (1990:313) found that work force characteristics such as the average educational level account for only a small portion of that variation. He also found that state unemployment rates are only weakly related to total employment growth. The factor that appears to have the greatest impact upon unemployment levels is the loss of high-wage jobs. The shift of employment away from high-wage industries such as manufacturing, construction, transportation, and public utilities has an especially strong impact. The loss of high-wage jobs in these industries results in prolonged unemployment spells and higher unemployment rates, and those rates fall only very gradually as the overall employment level rises. In other words, people are much more likely to enter the unemployment rolls as jobs are lost in high-wage industries than they are to leave those rolls as employment increases in low-wage industries.

The implications of this analysis differ markedly from those of turnover models of unemployment. The most effective way to reduce unemployment is to minimize the loss of high-wage jobs in the first place and to offset the loss that does occur with comparable employment opportunities. Unfortunately, the U.S. economy has been more successful of late at generating low-wage jobs than it has been at preventing the loss of high-wage employment. Stable macroeconomic policies would have avoided the sharp contraction in manufacturing employment in the 1980s, but macroeconomic policy alone will do little to lower the unemployment trend as long as most new jobs offer low wages. If we wish to lower unemployment and improve the inflation-unemployment trade-off, we have to raise the earnings ability of displaced workers.

NOTES

1.   The discussion of Keynes's contribution to our understanding of unemployment draws upon Wachtel (1992:281–83).

2.   Among the more influential analysts who developed a turnover explanation for the "new" unemployment of the 1970s were Robert Hall (1970, 1972) and Martin Feldstein (1973).

3.   The importance of the NAIRU for understanding the actions of the Federal Reserve is discussed in Krugman (1990:27–32).

4.   That is, when energy prices are excluded from the CPI (see Council of Economic Advisors 1988:81–84).

5.   Most of these studies were republished in Summers's *Understanding Unemployment* (1990).

6.   Multiplying the unemployment rates of various age groups by their labor force share reveals that the unemployment attributable to teenagers amounted to 1.2 percentage points in 1965 when the overall rate was 4.5 percent. It amounted to 1.3 percentage points in 1985 when the rate was 7.2 percent (see Summers 1990:297).

Toward an Active Labor Market Policy **III**

The Case for Worker Training 7

The future now belongs to societies that organize themselves for learning. . . . More than ever before, nations that want high incomes and full employment must develop policies that emphasize the acquisition of knowledge and skills by everyone, not just a select few.

—Ray Marshall and Marc Tucker, *Thinking for a Living: Education and the Wealth of Nations*

There is an emerging consensus on the need to improve the skills of American workers. As long as the real earnings of the average worker were rising, it was easy to overlook the failings of worker training programs. Today the typical male high school graduate makes considerably less than his counterpart earned twenty-five years ago, and the skill development of the work force has become a public issue. Workers' skills in this country are not considered equal to those of workers in Europe and Japan, and studies by various national commissions have begun to address the question of how to raise the skill level of an undertrained America.[1] The immediate concern is the skill level of current work force members. Nearly 90 percent of the people who will be working in the year 2000 are already in the work force. Ending the stagnation in earnings growth in the near future means improving their productivity, and that will require a greater investment in training.

The case for worker training begins with the changing demand for labor. New technologies, the movement toward a global economy, and shifts in consumer tastes have combined to reduce the earnings of those in routine jobs. Advances in transportation and communication have lowered shipping costs, enabled capital and technology to move rapidly across national borders, and opened the way for low-wage countries to produce high-volume, standardized goods. The barriers of distance that protected domestic markets from foreign competition have been breached. A growing percentage of merchandise production is entering world trade, and in a global economy the markets for mass-produced goods go to low-wage producers.

The increasing importance of skilled labor can also be traced to the product market and to changes in consumer demand. As real incomes rise, consumers become more discriminating with regard to product quality. They demand higher-quality goods that appeal to individual tastes. Firms

103

face more varied and fragmented markets, and price alone becomes less important in determining demand. High-quality goods and services that meet individual needs command a premium price and support higher wages, but to enter these markets firms must be able to compete on the basis of quality and to respond quickly to changing consumer tastes.

The saturation of markets for low-price, standardized goods and a more discriminating and differentiated demand on the part of consumers have combined to give a competitive advantage to firms that engage in what is often termed diversified, quality production. Diversified production is based upon the microelectronic and computer technologies that make short production runs for fragmented markets economically feasible, but these technologies need to be combined with new forms of work organization to realize their potential.[2] Small-batch production requires internal flexibility and constant adjustment. Employees need to communicate more often and with more people in order to adjust their jobs to changes in the schedule and content of production. As decision-making responsibility diffuses throughout the workplace, it transforms the organization of work and the skill content of jobs. Case studies of both manufacturing and service industries consistently find that flexible production systems foster participation and greater reliance upon worker skills (Benton, Bailey, Noyelle, and Stanback 1991). They demonstrate the importance of a highly skilled and motivated work force.

By transforming the organization of the workplace, diversified, quality production raises skill levels and increases the need for training. The mass production of standardized goods for the lowest possible price requires only a small number of highly skilled workers in management and planning departments that are often physically separate and remote from the actual production sites. It is a form of production that is compatible with highly centralized, vertically integrated organizations. In contrast, the diversified production of goods and services designed to meet the specific needs of customers argues for decentralized, functionally integrated organizations (Streek 1993). Those directly involved in producing goods or providing services necessarily assume responsibility for managerial and support functions such as scheduling, quality control, and maintenance. Integrating these functions into the production process improves productivity and product quality, but it demands a high degree of competence on the part of the work force and a large supply of overlapping skills. Individual employees must perform a wide variety of tasks, and they must understand and be able to adjust to the work of others. As changes in the product market give rise to decentralized and functionally integrated organizations, these organizational changes create a need for higher levels of worker competence and skill.

The case for worker training thus highlights the way in which the demands of rapidly changing product markets are transforming the workplace. As product lives shorten, as the number of new products increases, and as production operations become more complex, new forms of work organization emerge. Reduced response time and worker responsibility for product quality become the hallmarks of successful organizations, and basic literacy and numeracy skills offer greater returns in the form of productivity and earnings. Evidence of the increasing return on skills can be seen in labor force surveys. Even among workers with the same educational attainment, elementary math skills were twice as important in explaining wage differences in 1986 as in 1978, just eight years earlier (Murnane and Levy 1994:76).

* * * *

The case for increased training is compelling, but it is not being widely acted upon in this country. Comparing expenditures on "staff development" across countries is complicated by different accounting procedures and by differences in what gets counted as training. Nonetheless, it is evident that European and Japanese firms typically spend a higher percentage of payroll on training than U.S. companies, and that most of their training expenditure is devoted to production and nonsupervisory workers.[3] The United States is exceptional for the small percentage of the nonsupervisory work force that gets company training. Only a few percent of young workers who are not college graduates receive formal training from their employer. The weak commitment to training on the part of U.S. firms is clearly revealed by comparing specific industries. The average auto worker in a Japanese or Japanese-owned U.S. plant receives two to three times the amount of training as an auto workers in a U.S.-owned plant. The difference is even greater among new hires, who spend three hundred hours in training in Japanese-owned plants, compared to forty-eight hours in U.S. plants (Lynch 1994:71–74). Throughout American industry, firms limit their training expenditure upon nonsupervisory workers either by continuing highly routinized production operations that require little training or by relying upon the external labor market for needed skills. For all the pronouncements on the importance of knowledge-driven growth, U.S. companies provide little training for the majority of their employees.

It is not surprising that employers who maintain traditional forms of work organization based upon routine job assignments, low pay, and high turnover see little need for a more highly skilled work force and feel little pressure to invest in worker training. What is surprising is that the demand for training remains comparatively weak even though a majority of the larger U.S. companies have instituted quality control circles, total quality management, team-based production, or some combination of the three (Hammonds, Kelly, and Thurston 1994). Most employers are concerned that their employees exhibit a good work ethic and appropriate social behavior, and they usually require a high school diploma as a way of screening for those qualities. Yet the Commission on the Skills of the American Work Force (1990) found that only a small percentage of employers express concern over skills shortages within the work force or make more than a token investment in training their non-college-educated workers.

The hesitancy of U.S. employers to invest in worker training cannot be attributed simply to the persistence of traditional forms of work organization. We may question the strength of their commitment to change, but many companies are restructuring and evolving more functionally integrated organizations as they downsize. What they are not doing is retraining the employees whose jobs are made redundant by this reorganization. In a 1984 survey, only 36 percent of the senior personnel managers of Fortune 1500 companies reported a policy of retraining employees when their current jobs are eliminated, and this percentage does not appear to have increased substantially (Rosow and Zager 1988:6–9). Since these large firms usually follow more progressive personnel practices than smaller companies, the overall percentage that retrains is much lower. Most companies follow a policy of hire and fire. They calculate that it is less costly to dismiss employees as their jobs become redundant and to hire workers with the needed skills as new positions are created.

These hire-and-fire policies are not cost free. The monetary costs of dismissals, which may include severance pay, unemployment compensation, and "bumping" costs, have been estimated to average eight or nine thousand dollars, while the cost of retraining employees for new positions is usually much less (Rosow and Zager 1988:201). In addition to these monetary costs, terminations disrupt work routines, undermine employee loyalty and motivation, and create increased resistance to change on the part of those fearful of losing their jobs. A policy of hire and fire is not likely to elicit the willingness to think on the job that is the hallmark of diversified, quality production. Without some assurance of job security, employees have little reason to acquire specific skills, to contribute ideas, or to maintain a high performance standard. Apparently, most employers have concluded that these costs are outweighed by the benefit of being able to adjust staffing levels quickly through layoffs and dismissals.

Training produces a more skilled and adaptable work force, but it does not confer greater flexibility over staffing levels. On the contrary, employers who provide training are less likely to resort to layoffs and dismissals for fear of losing trained employees. Stable employment relationships also make training more effective because workers are more willing to invest time and energy acquiring specific skills. The benefits of training and job security are mutually reinforcing. Training gives employers an incentive to retain workers, and employment stability motivates workers to learn. If employers are hesitant to train, it is because they cannot or will not provide the kind of employment assurances that make training worthwhile.

Firms are especially hesitant to invest in general skills training that improves worker competencies across a wide range of job tasks and occupations. Portable skills increase the value of employees to other firms. They raise the possibility that competing firms will bid trained employees away before the firm doing the training can recoup its investment. The more general the training, therefore, the more the benefits of that training accrue to individuals in the form of increased mobility and higher wages, and the more they will be expected to bear the training costs. Individuals usually pay for general skills training by receiving a lower training wage. The problem is that most workers are hesitant to accept a lower wage where there is no assurance of continued employment and no way of certifying the vocational skills that they will supposedly acquire.

Changes in the product market or even in the organization of the workplace will not compel employers and workers to invest in training where they do not perceive that training investment to be in their interest. There is no organizational imperative that will inevitably compel rational employers to invest in the skills of their workers. In this country, training is regarded as primarily an individual responsibility, and employers see little to be gained from sharing in that responsibility. Our labor market institutions only weakly sanction layoffs and dismissals, and high rates of worker turnover make it difficult for employers to capture the returns on general skills training. The best training strategy for individual firms, therefore, is not to train. They adapt to changes in demand by adjusting staffing levels and by relying upon the external labor market for needed skills. In essence, they seek greater flexibility through a policy of hire and fire or of layoff and recall even though the result is an undertrained work force.

Other industrial countries impose greater penalties upon firms that resort to layoffs and dismissals. Their labor market institutions reward employment stability. Employers adjust to changes in the product market through a more flexible use of labor within the workplace, and training is the key to that kind of flexibility. They are also less likely to dismiss or lay off workers during business downturns and thus are better able to capture the return on training. The remainder of this chapter explores these differences by describing some of the labor market policies that promote worker training in other industrial countries. These alternative training strategies are then contrasted with our fragmented and largely ineffective federally funded programs and with the limited and highly specific training provided through state-sponsored programs. These contrasts underscore the need for a more coherent and universal training system that conforms to national standards for program evaluation and skill certification.

CHARACTERISTICS OF ALTERNATIVE TRAINING SYSTEMS

While U.S. firms benefited from a huge and relatively protected domestic market, European and Japanese firms, operating within smaller, export-oriented economies, were long exposed to the pressures of international trade. Those trade pressures and the devastation of their economies during the Second World War forged a collective awareness of the connection between a skilled work force and national prosperity. The national effort to rebuild shattered economies and the effort to regain export markets were linked and help to explain why the Germans and Japanese, in particular, were quick to appreciate the importance of competing on the basis of productivity and product quality. These historic contrasts also help to explain the broad public support in Europe and Japan for a more active government role in developing training institutions.

The foremost example of a government-led approach to training is Sweden, and public support has been crucial to the success of its active labor market policy. The basic premise of that policy is that unemployment should be combated through job placement and training and that passive measures such as unemployment compensation should be used as a last resort. Sweden adopted this policy in the 1950s when Gosta Rehn and Rudolph Meidner, economists with the Swedish Federation of Labor, called for a comprehensive system of employment and training programs to control inflationary pressures without higher unemployment. By the mid-1980s Sweden was spending two-thirds of its labor market budget, about 3 percent of GNP, on employment and training programs, and the number of workers enrolled in those programs exceeded the number officially unemployed.[4]

Like every market, the labor market functions best when there is competition based upon full and accurate information. Employers need information about the available pool of applicants and about the qualifications of individual workers, and job-seekers need to be informed about the requirements and rewards of available jobs. Recognizing the importance of information to the operation of the market, countries like Sweden and Denmark have made the public employment service the center of their labor market systems. The employment service gathers information not only to place workers, but also to identify skill shortages and to coordinate training programs designed to supply needed skills. To better enable these services to forecast occupational demand, employers are required to list job vacancies, and in some countries the public employment service has a near monopoly on organized job placement. In Sweden, for example, private employment agencies are not allowed to operate. In other European countries as well, the public employment service has legal access to job listings and operates as an umbrella organization for placement and training programs that meet national standards and skill classifications. Qualified job-seekers are matched to available jobs and helped to relocate when necessary. Those who are not qualified receive training at little or no expense, and family income supports are available while wage earners undergo training. The employment service thus provides the information crucial to labor market performance: information about the requirements of jobs, about the qualifications of job-seekers, and about the training needed to qualify people for available jobs.

These employment and training programs are obviously costly, but they are defended on the grounds that they improve the trade-off between inflation and unemployment. They are designed to keep inflation low and employment high by reducing the structural unemployment that typically occurs when there is an oversupply of people trained for jobs that are no longer in demand and a shortage of people trained for the occupations that are in demand. As wages rise in response to the labor shortages in certain occupations and areas, structural unemployment and inflation will coexist in the same economy. Training or relocating job-seekers to fill these labor shortages alleviates inflationary pressures. Providing skills that are in short supply speeds the reallocation of labor from contracting to expanding sectors, reduces structural unemployment, and improves the inflation-unemployment trade-off. Sweden's active labor market policies in particular are based upon the belief that it is more efficient and less wasteful of human resources to control inflation by increasing the supply of skilled workers than by creating unemployment (see Marshall and Tucker 1992).

An active labor market policy is not limited to training and relocation assistance. Temporary relief work and public service jobs cushion the impact of unemployment in depressed areas and industries and help to maintain the earnings and self-confidence of the unemployed. Still, the key to Sweden's labor market system is the use of the national employment service to provide good labor market information and to oversee the public investment in worker training. Its government-led programs alleviate the reemployment problems of displaced workers and improve economic efficiency by eliminating skill mismatches. Of course, this approach assumes that structural imbalances in the economy are the major source of worker dislocation and the primary justification for training.

An alternative strategy seeks to improve the job performance and earnings ability of those still employed and emphasizes company-based training as the most effective means of achieving that goal. There are a variety of ways in which other industrial countries promote employer-based training. The Japanese government directly subsidizes in-house training. Japanese firms also form long-term relationships with specific schools, whose students they recruit for production jobs. The schools concentrate on basic literacy, math, and communication skills, and students know that their performance will determine the kind of job they obtain. Japanese firms then build upon these foundation skills with programs that include a large component of general training. They are willing to do this because there is little employee turnover. Firms rarely resort to layoffs during business downturns, and employees who leave voluntarily usually incur large wage losses. Workers have a powerful incentive to remain with an employer because the wage increases associated with tenure are four times greater in Japan than in the United States (Lynch 1994:65).

France and Australia, along with Singapore and a few other countries, promote employer-financed training through a payroll tax. In France it is a "play or pay" tax, which applies to all firms with ten or more employees. Employers who cannot certify that their training expenditures amount to at least 1.4 percent of payroll must pay the difference into a publicly administered fund. That fund is then supposed to provide training for the employees of firms that do not implement their own program. The tax assures a uniform level of training investment on the part of firms and lessens the tendency to bid away trained employees, but the evidence to date suggests that unskilled workers and the employees of small companies do not receive their share of training benefits.[5]

Perhaps the most ambitious effort to encourage employer-provided training is Germany's apprenticeship program. The vast majority of German students who do not attend a university (and many who eventually do) enter apprenticeships that include classroom training in general skill areas. The unions, through their representation on the works councils that exist within most German firms, have worked to assure that the vocational skills acquired through these apprenticeships conform to national standards. The programs are also certified by local chambers of commerce that discourage the hiring of trained apprentices by firms that did not provide the training. Most apprentices stay with the company that trains them, but even where there is turnover apprentices are motivated to learn because they receive certified skills that will lead to a high-paying job. The result is a virtuous circle. Apprentices are willing to accept a training wage that is much lower than that of unskilled adult workers. And because the training wage is so low, firms are anxious to hire apprentices and willing to invest in general skills training. The institutional supports for Germany's apprenticeship program illustrate why it is difficult for a single firm to increase the training it offers its employees (Lynch 1994). If a firm offers training in the absence of national skill standards and certification, workers will demand a higher wage. If the firm then pays for the general training that it offers, it risks losing that investment should its trained employees then leave. The best strategy, therefore, is not to train or to train in highly specific areas. The result is an inadequately trained work force even though individual firms would train more if other firms would do the same. By providing nationally certified skills, Germany's apprenticeship program overcomes this market failure and raises the level of skill development throughout the work force.

THE HISTORY OF FEDERALLY FUNDED TRAINING
IN THE UNITED STATES

The U.S. Employment Service (USES) was created during the 1930s as part of the unemployment insurance system. Unlike the employment services in other industrial countries, USES was never granted a legal right to private job listings. Administrative authority over its two thousand offices is delegated to individual states; it competes ineffectively against private employment agencies; and its services are rarely coordinated with other labor market programs. Few job vacancies are even listed with USES. The percentage of all job vacancies listed with the service, the vacancy penetration rate, declined from roughly 18 percent in the 1960s to about 12 percent in the 1980s. The percentage of all job vacancies that it fills, the placement rate, is even lower and shows a similar decline (Janoski 1990:103). Most employers regard USES as part of an income transfer system that is irrelevant to their personnel needs. They are rarely involved in developing or monitoring its screening and referral procedures, and they usually list only menial job openings with the service.

Lacking a stable organizational base in a national employment service, federally funded training programs are usually implemented on a project or ad hoc basis. Providing skills training for the entire work force has never been a public policy goal in this country, but programs for specific groups of displaced and disadvantaged workers can be traced to the Manpower Development and Training Act (MDTA) of 1962. MDTA was originally intended to retrain workers displaced by technological change, but it was redirected to offer remedial and skills training to the urban poor as part of the Johnson administration's War on Poverty. The ostensible goal of the program was to reduce poverty and to improve the operation of the labor market by augmenting the human capital of the least-skilled workers.

This training effort was not without success. The creation of the Job Corps in 1964 removed many young people from poor neighborhood environments and placed them in residential centers where peer pressure, as well as skill training and work experience, could effect a change in outlook. The Job Corps experience had a positive impact upon the subsequent work histories of many young people, and it is regarded as an effective youth employment program. Unfortunately, many of the adult training programs that originated with MDTA have not been as successful.

Federally funded training programs were consolidated under the Comprehensive Employment and Training Act (CETA) of 1973. CETA was passed as part of the Nixon administration's New Federalism, and it began the process of shifting administrative responsibility for job training to the states and localities. The legislation established local prime sponsors who then submitted training proposals to Washington, but the training programs that were created appear to have had a very limited impact upon area job markets. Most of the programs were means-tested, or available only to individuals whose incomes fall below some predetermined level, and they came to be viewed as part of the welfare system. As a result, participants were often stigmatized in the eyes of potential employers, who regarded the training offered as largely irrelevant to their needs. In a review of the CETA programs, the Congressional Budget Office (1982:6) estimated their benefit-cost ratio to be about one. That is, the discounted benefit of higher future earnings for program trainees was roughly equal to the cost of running the programs. Most of the effect upon earnings was the result of increased labor force participation. CETA training was associated with an increase in the number of hours worked, especially among female participants, but it had little impact upon hourly wage rates. The programs offered hope and confidence, as well as basic job search skills, to individuals with very little work experience, but they did not improve the earnings ability of most participants.

The CETA legislation also provided public service employment for specified categories of workers. Public service jobs are often criticized for their substitution effects, by which it is usually meant that they displace actual or potential private-sector jobs. In the case of CETA, it was claimed that federal funds were being used to pay for work that the states and localities would have paid for out of their own revenues, thereby shifting the local tax burden to the federal government without creating any additional jobs. Although substitution effects are always a theoretical possibility, their actual magnitude in the case of CETA was never established. But when the Carter administration used public service employment as a countercyclical measure, increasing the number of public service jobs from 300,000 to 750,000 in just nine months, criticism rapidly escalated. Sar Levitan and Frank Gallo have described the result:

> [T]he pressure to quickly fill these jobs resulted in isolated, though highly publicized, cases of careless management and enrollment of ineligible applicants that were to haunt CETA for the rest of its limited life. (1988:9)

CETA's public service jobs reduced local unemployment rates and provided work experience to hundreds of thousands of disadvantaged individuals, but the program never enjoyed popular support and could not be defended against the opposition of the Reagan administration. Expenditures on public service employment were cut and then eliminated in 1981. The CETA legislation itself expired the following year with the country in the midst of a severe recession. House Democrats tried to revive public service employment in hopes of cushioning the impact of the recession, but they abandoned that effort as part of a compromise that reauthorized federal funding for training programs under the Jobs Training Partnership Act (JTPA) of 1982. As its title suggests, the JTPA legislation was designed to promote closer cooperation between the various levels of government and the private sector.[6] Under JTPA, administrative oversight of federally funded training programs became the responsibility of state governors, who were required to issue performance standards for evaluating the success or failure of their individual state's programs. Congress had intended for the federal government to monitor state and local compliance with the act and to evaluate as well as fund these training programs, but its intention was thwarted. The Reagan administration expressed its disapproval of public training initiatives by treating JTPA as a block grant program and neglecting its responsibilities under the act. Representative Augustus Hawkins aptly characterized the administration's response when he observed that "[t]he federal government put the money on a stump and ran away" (quoted in Levitan and Gallo 1988:18).

This lack of federal involvement in program administration, rather than demonstrating the potential of state leadership, is thought to have contributed to its failure. Most states failed to establish priorities for their JTPA programs and limited their role to meeting the minimum requirements of the act. There has been little or no effort to coordinate JTPA programs with the state-run employment services or with other social programs, even though the act called for such coordination. Decision-making was delegated to local service delivery areas (SDAs), where elected officials and private industry councils (PICs) jointly appoint program administrators and choose service providers. Granting administrative authority to the PICs is credited with making the programs more acceptable to local business groups, but there is no evidence that worker training under JTPA has been any more effective than it was under CETA.

In addition to prohibiting the creation of public service jobs, the JTPA legislation severely restricted the amount of income support available to trainees. Both the Title II programs for disadvantaged job-seekers and the Title III programs for displaced workers required that 70 percent of all funding be spent on training and that the remaining 30 percent cover all support services and administrative costs. This restriction reduced costs and limited program enrollment by effectively excluding many eligible participants who needed income support while undergoing training. The act also called for the use of numerical performance standards in contracting and program evaluation. Under performance-based contracting, the payments to training providers are usually made contingent upon their meeting specific job placement goals. Although performance standards represent a form of accountability, they encourage trainers to select participants and to restrict the kind of employment services offered. Service providers are paid on the basis of how many trainees are quickly placed, so they screen eligible participants and enroll only those whom they consider most employable. Case studies of the most "successful" JTPA programs found that many potential enrollees were required to engage in preliminary job search, and only those who reported job leads or offers were then enrolled. This practice of "creaming" limits participation and tends to exclude the high school dropouts and older workers who most need training. For example, more than three million individuals were displaced from their jobs in 1985, yet only a little over 220,000 were enrolled in some 500 JTPA projects. Roughly a quarter of these projects did not enroll workers over the age of fifty-four, and one in nine excluded those without a high school diploma (Levitan and Gallo 1988:114–15).

Funding restrictions and superficial performance standards geared to rapid job placement also altered the mix of program services offered under JTPA. A nationwide survey conducted by the General Accounting Office and covering all Title III projects through March 1985 found that only 26 percent of participants received classroom training and only 6 percent were enrolled in remedial skills classes, while more than 80 percent received job search assistance (Levitan and Gallo 1988:117–18). The emphasis upon job search assistance is considered cost effective because the cost per placement is much less than that of on-the-job or classroom training. The implicit goal of most programs is to move participants into available jobs as quickly as possible with little regard to their future earnings on those jobs.

The evolution of federal employment and training policy toward locally administered programs built around modest, short-term investments in job search assistance continued with the passage of the Economic Dislocation and Worker Adjustment Act (EDWAA) in 1988. EDWAA amended Title III of JTPA to require that 80 percent of all program funds go to the states and that 60 percent of these state funds be transferred to the local SDAs. It also stipulated that no more than 25 percent of the funds be spent on income support for those served. In addition, EDWAA combined Title III of JTPA with the Trade Adjustment Assistance (TAA) program, which provides income support to workers certified to have lost their jobs as a result of import competition. By signing up for job search assistance, those qualifying can receive up to a year of benefits. TAA thus offers partial compensation to some of those who bear the costs of labor market adjustment, but it is not considered an effective training program. A 1993 internal report prepared by the Department of Labor found that one-half of all TAA recipients did not even enroll for training and that only one-fifth were placed in jobs that paid at least 80 percent of their former wage (Kilborn 1993).

EVALUATING PUBLIC TRAINING PROGRAMS

There have been numerous evaluations of the CETA and JTPA programs. Unfortunately, it has been difficult to reach firm conclusions about the effectiveness of the training offered because of methodological problems with the studies. The evaluations that were done of the CETA program did not incorporate an experimental design, and their estimates of the impact of training upon worker earnings were often biased (see Barnow 1987). A nationwide, experimental study of the JTPA program was carried out by the Department of Labor in the late 1980s, but it was unable to obtain a representative sample of program sites. Most program administrators refused to participate because of the ethical and practical issues involved in denying assistance to the participants who were randomly assigned to control groups (Hotz 1992). Probably the best assessments of publicly funded worker training programs come from a series of demonstration projects that evaluated the services provided to displaced workers. Several of these projects lacked a true experimental design, but the largest, the New Jersey Unemployment Insurance Reemployment Demonstration Project (NJUIRDP), conducted an experimental study of ten randomly selected sites within that state's unemployment insurance (UI) system. It presents an accurate assessment of the limited effectiveness of our public training programs.

NJUIRDP was a joint project of the United States and New Jersey Departments of Labor that ran from July 1986 to June 1987.[7] The project goal was to use the UI system to identify displaced workers who are likely to experience long unemployment spells, and then to assess the effectiveness of various treatments in speeding their return to work. Roughly one-quarter of the UI claimants at the ten sites, a total of more than ten thousand individuals, were identified as being at risk of remaining unemployed for a long period and were randomly assigned either to one of three treatments or to a control group. All of the claimants assigned to a treatment group received a set of services that comprised the job search assistance treatment, and failure to report for these services could have resulted in denial of UI benefits. The first treatment consisted of these services. The second treatment offered classroom or on-the-job training in addition to job search assistance. This offer was accepted by only 15 percent of those assigned to the treatment. The third treatment combined job search assistance with a reemployment bonus that gradually decreased in amount with the time spent out of work. Finally, to avoid denying assistance to any claimant, the control group was eligible for all JTPA Title III programs. The demonstration thus compared each treatment to the existing service environment.

The NJUIRDP evaluations found that the treatments resulted in earlier reemployment and a significant reduction in the amount of UI benefits collected. These results occurred within two years of program completion and were attributed to the job search assistance. None of the treatments had a significant long-term impact upon the number of weeks worked or upon the participants' earnings. Those who received classroom or on-the-job training reported considerably higher earnings, but so few participants had elected to undergo this training that the differences were not statistically significant. NJUIRDP thus demonstrated that it is possible to build linkages between the employment service and worker training programs, as the JTPA legislation had intended. Yet for all the sophistication of its research design, the project basically reaffirmed the findings of earlier evaluations: Job search assistance speeds up the reemployment process, reduces expenditures on UI benefits, and is cost-effective. Although earlier reemployment results in increased earnings, the significance of the earnings gain diminishes rapidly over time. Classroom and on-the-job training, which should improve earnings ability over the long-term, do not add significantly to the gains from job search assistance and are not cost effective.

Evaluation projects such as NJUIRDP do not prove that skills training cannot be effective. They show that without access to private job listings it is very difficult to develop training curricula that provide marketable skills. Given the very low participation rate and the short duration of the training, they also show that most programs are too small and too brief to have a measurable impact on participant earnings. The basic problem lies in what the evaluators are evaluating: a complex and fragmented array of programs that pass for a training system. We should not expect to demonstrate the benefits of training where the institutional linkages and supports that make training effective do not exist.

STATE-SPONSORED TRAINING PROGRAMS

Our federally funded employment and training programs exhibit a number of weaknesses. The employment service lacks access to most private job listings and fills few job vacancies. Its ability to gather labor market information and to forecast skill shortages is correspondingly limited. Administrative control over the training programs is delegated to local officials with little direction or leadership from the federal or state governments. There is little coordination between these locally administered programs and the employment service, and there are no national standards that guide program development or certify the skills of participants. Training is restricted to specific categories of disadvantaged or displaced workers, and it usually has little impact upon their future earnings. Consequently, the program emphasis has shifted from training to job search assistance, from skill development to rapid reemployment in whatever jobs are available.

These weaknesses of the public employment and training system have led many states to develop training programs that better address their economic development goals. Some of the most effective training in this country is being offered through state programs that train or retrain the employees of resident firms. Most of these programs originated in the beggar-thy-neighbor economic development strategies of competing states, and they continue to be used as locational incentives to lure or retain mobile firms. However, the training offered is usually effective because the programs originate in response to employer requests and are designed to meet their training needs.

Paul Osterman and Rosemary Batt (1993) describe the two ways in which state-funded training is usually delivered. The more common method is to set up separate agencies that offer customized training to individual firms. The largest and best-known example of this agency-based approach is California's Employment Training Panel (ETP). In operation since 1983, California's ETP approves only programs that are designed in response to specific proposals from employers. The training is preceded by a contract specifying the curriculum to be used, and the employers must make a commitment to hire or retain those trained. During its first nine years of operation, ETP approved 1,200 training contracts for programs that enrolled 198,000 trainees and that cost between $2,000 and $3,500 for each participant. A different approach is exemplified by the community colleges of North and South Carolina, which, in addition to their regular degree programs, contract to offer specialized training courses for individual employers. Instead of administering training programs through separate agencies, North Carolina consolidated all of its programs, including JTPA, within its community college system. One of those programs, the New and Expanding Industries Program, trained over 210,000 workers for more than 2,400 companies between 1963 and 1989 (Osterman and Batt 1993:470–74).

Even though the skills it provides are beneficial to both workers and firms, employer-centered training has a number of drawbacks. First and foremost, it tends to exclude displaced and disadvantaged workers. State officials are quick to differentiate the economic development goals of the training they offer from what they consider to be the social welfare objectives of federally funded programs like JTPA. Most of the funds provided through state initiatives such as California's ETP are used to retrain the current employees of large companies.[8] This funding priority obviously underserves displaced workers, but female, minority, and less-educated workers are also underrepresented among the current employees of large corporations. Community college programs differ somewhat from agency-based training in this regard. Because of their dual education and training function, they enroll a more diverse group of trainees. But whether training is provided through separate state agencies or through the community college system, the contracts with training vendors are usually performance based, and workers with weak educational backgrounds tend to be excluded. Performance-based contracting led to creaming in the JTPA programs as well, but state-funded programs are not targeted to disadvantaged groups to begin with, and they are less likely to help those most in need of assistance.

A related drawback to state-sponsored programs is that they often subsidize training that private employers would otherwise have financed on their own. It is difficult for state officials to determine beforehand whether the training assistance sought by employers will result in additional hires or will avoid layoffs, and there is always a risk that the programs simply substitute public for private training expenditures. This risk can be minimized by targeting assistance to small and at-risk firms that are unlikely to provide training on their own, but a better way to address this problem is by regulating the kind of training that is funded. Subsidizing training is most objectionable when the skills being learned are specific to the firm. To ensure that the training provided emphasizes general skills, the curricula should be based upon national standards and skill classifications. Training that conforms to national skill standards benefits the larger society as well as the recipient workers and firms.

A final drawback to these state programs is that they too are often implemented on an ad hoc or project basis and therefore fail to correct the organizational weaknesses of the current training system. Too little effort is given to developing permanent linkages between training agencies, employer and community associations, and individual firms. Lauri Bassi's (1994) description of the experience of firms that are currently providing their employees with general training in reading, writing, math, and English as a second language highlights this problem. Most of these firms were under pressure to improve the quality of their products by incorporating techniques such as statistical quality control into the production process, and they wanted to insure that their employees had the general literacy and math skills needed to adjust to these changes. The biggest obstacles they encountered were the uncertainty and start-up costs associated with designing appropriate curricula and finding effective trainers. Once the programs were ongoing, the average cost of the training per employee was about six hundred dollars, an amount considered reasonably low. Most employers financed at least part of this direct cost and all contributed indirectly by providing release time from work. Contrary to what we might expect, there was no evidence that training costs were passed on to workers through wage or benefits reductions, and only a small fraction of the employers interviewed felt that their training investment had resulted in increased worker turnover. A majority cited higher worker morale and loyalty as important benefits of the programs.

There was also general agreement among the employers with regard to the kind of public assistance that would elicit a greater training investment on their part. More than financial subsidies, they wanted technical assistance with program start-up and with the design of effective curricula, and they wanted information about programs and trainers that had been used by other firms. Smaller employers were particularly anxious for assistance in creating associations that would disseminate information and lower their average training costs by enabling them to contract jointly with trainers. In short, they perceived a need for a training system that would make information more available, while minimizing the risks and start-up costs associated with new programs.

The drawbacks of state-sponsored programs reveal the need for a better-coordinated training system that conforms to national guidelines and standards. We need a labor market system that disseminates information about the value of training, about the costs of training, and about how to train. Above all, we need a system that gives employers an incentive to invest in the general skills of their employees, an investment that would greatly benefit less-educated and low-income workers without being targeted exclusively to them. What we have are federally funded programs that seek to quickly reemploy displaced or disadvantaged workers in whatever jobs are available, and state-sponsored programs that serve primarily to retrain the employees of large companies, often subsidizing firm-specific training in the process.

CREATING INCENTIVES TO TRAIN

To improve the earnings ability of the average worker, more skills and knowledge need to be incorporated into the goods and services we produce. That will require new forms of work organization and a greater training investment on the part of employers, and these changes will not occur in response to market forces alone. The best training strategy for any individual firm depends upon what other firms are doing. It therefore depends upon the institutional incentives and constraints that all firms face.

An important institutional support for training in many European countries is the high percentage of the work force that is unionized. As long as firms compete through low wages and routinized job assignments, no training system is going to be effective. By defending against wage cuts and by imposing a uniform wage pattern upon unionized industries, unions take wages out of competition while pushing employers to increase productivity. In addition, the unions in countries such as Germany have begun to bargain over the amount and content of training. Collective-bargaining agreements that obligate employers to train are then extended to all of the firms within an industry, which means that they take the costs of training out of competition as well. The unions in this country could broaden their traditional role and bargain for increased training just as they bargain for higher wages. Unfortunately, unions here represent less than 12 percent of the private-sector work force, and they have organized only a small fraction of the smaller companies that are least likely to train. Reversing the decline in union density and developing new forms of employee representation are important goals in their own right, but expanding union membership rolls would also help to ensure a more effective training system.

Another institutional change that would lead to increased training is the imposition of a payroll tax. The Commission on the Skills of the American Work Force (1990) recommended that all employers, regardless of size or type of business, be required to spend at least 1 percent of payroll on certified education and training programs. Those companies unable or unwilling to develop in-house training programs would pay into a publicly administered fund that would provide training for their employees. What makes this training incentive so attractive is its apparent simplicity. It raises the level of training without creating a large government-run program. Firms simply certify on their tax returns, subject to audit, that they have made the required expenditure on training. However, without a union or employee organization to monitor the reported expenditures there is no guarantee that they will benefit those most in need of training or be used to raise the general skill level of the work force. The imposition of a payroll tax may increase training expenditures, but in France it did not ensure that unskilled workers and those in smaller firms received their share of training benefits.

A more ambitious institutional reform would be the creation of a system of apprenticeships for young people who do not plan to go to college and who are willing to invest in accredited vocational skills. Training programs that conform to national standards and provide nationally certified skills give younger workers an incentive to accept lower wages during the training period. In turn, firms that pay apprentices lower wages are more willing to provide both general and specific training. Once that training is completed, employers who wish to retain skilled employees and realize the full benefit of their investment will have to raise those wages.

Providing employers with incentives to train is not enough. It does not eliminate the need for a national employment service with greater access to private job listings, for training agencies that contract with firms individually or collectively to provide technical and organizational assistance, or for programs that assist disadvantaged workers. But we cannot create an effective training system as long as employers have little incentive to participate. Employer participation is essential if we are to move toward a universal training system that is capable of winning broad public support. As a rule, the greater the percentage of the populace that benefits from a program, the greater the public support that it enjoys. Labor market policies that benefit the majority of workers are easier to defend and more likely to be effective. When program eligibility is needs based or otherwise restricted to certain categories of individuals, it is viewed as part of the welfare system, and program participants are stigmatized. Training programs that lack the support of a broad constituency are also highly vulnerable to funding cuts and termination. The effort to influence the operation of the labor market by targeting assistance to limited categories of workers has proved to be ineffective and unsustainable. It is time to broaden that effort.

NOTES

1.   Over a decade ago the National Commission on Excellence in Education addressed the need to improve worker skills in *A Nation at Risk: The Imperative for Educational Reform* (1983). More recently, the Commission on the Skills of the American Work Force sounded a similar alarm in *America's Choice: High Skills or Low Wages* (1990).

2.   Michael Piore and Charles Sabel's *The Second Industrial Divide* (1984) presents a classic exposition of the changing relationship between consumer demand, industry structure, and the organization of work.

3.   The Commission on the Skills of the American Work Force (1990:49, 62) found that fewer than two hundred U.S. firms spend as much as 2 percent of payroll on training and less than one-third of the total private training expenditure benefits workers who do not have a college degree. By comparison, many European and Japanese firms spend as much as 6 percent of payroll on training, and most of this expenditure is used to train nonsupervisory workers.

4.   Sweden's active labor market policies are described in Marshall (1989) and Marshall and Tucker (1992:218–21).

5.   In 1972, French firms with twenty to forty-nine employees spent 0.62 percent of payroll on training compared to an average expenditure of 2.5 percent by firms with two thousand or more employees. By 1984 the gap had widened to 1.22 and 3.45 percent of payroll, respectively (Osterman and Batt 1993:469).

6.   This description of the JTPA legislation and programs is based upon Levitan and Gallo (1988).

7.   The design and findings of the NJUIRDP project are reported in Anderson, Corson, and Decker (1990).

8.   About 90 percent of California's ETP funds are used to retrain current employees (Osterman and Batt 1993:471).

Work Sharing and Job Security ————————————— 8

> One of the great ironies of our present situation is that overwork for the majority has been accompanied by the growth of enforced idleness for the minority.
>
> —Juliet Schor, *The Overworked American: The Unexpected Decline of Leisure*

The U.S. record of employment growth is impressive compared to that of other industrial countries. Unfortunately, our success at job creation has come at a high price. American workers are much more likely than their European or Japanese counterparts to be laid off or displaced, with all the personal hardships that this entails. Our per capita income is comparatively high, but it will not remain so if the recent rates of productivity and earnings growth persist. And no other advanced industrial country has experienced a comparable increase in earnings inequality in recent years. The combination of slow income growth and increased wage dispersion has produced a sharp decline in the living standards of low-wage workers and a sharp increase in poverty. Improving the earnings ability of less-skilled workers will require improved education and training, particularly company-based training, yet Americans receive less training from their employers than workers in Europe and Japan. Most of what is provided is targeted to those with a college education. Finally, it is no coincidence that the vast majority of workers in this country lack any form of collective representation at the workplace.

Our success in greatly adding to the employment rolls during the 1970s and 1980s is often credited to a flexible and little-regulated labor market. We experienced higher average unemployment during this period, but millions of additional American workers found jobs. Over the same period employment growth in Europe stagnated, and this lack of success at creating jobs and employing more of its citizens was often blamed upon the labor market effects of job protection practices and a comparatively generous social welfare system. In an effort to stimulate job growth many European countries began in the mid-1980s to cut unemployment compensation and social welfare spending, to privatize government-owned enterprises, and to eliminate or weaken many job protection measures (Blank and Freeman

1994). To date, this public retrenchment has done little to lower unemployment.[1] Meanwhile, the performance of the U.S. economy appears less impressive. Employment growth here slowed after the mid-1980s, came to a virtual halt during the recent recession, and has since resumed at a fairly modest pace, largely because of changing demographic trends. In addition, the real wages of most American workers continued to fall through the early years of this decade, and wage inequalities continued to worsen.

The argument that the employment problems of advanced industrial countries are the result of an overregulated labor market is less compelling today than it was a decade ago. Nonetheless, the opposition to a more active labor market policy in this country remains strong. This opposition is usually justified in terms of economic efficiency. It is argued that any intervention in a well-functioning market will distort the incentives that govern the behavior of economic actors and produce less efficient outcomes and a net loss of social welfare. For example, efforts to enhance economic security through unemployment insurance and social welfare programs raise wage expectations and affect the employment decision. These interventions are criticized for subsidizing longer unemployment spells, which represent potential losses of economic output and worker income. Similarly, efforts to enhance job security by constraining the ability of employers to dismiss workers slow the adjustment of employment levels to changes in labor demand and thereby affect hiring decisions. Job protection measures that raise the cost of dismissals also raise the cost of new hires and are criticized for impeding employment growth. Employers who cannot easily dismiss workers during business downturns will hire fewer workers than they otherwise would when business conditions improve. Again, the presumed result is higher unemployment and potential losses of output and income.

The preceding chapter presented a counterargument to these efficiency claims by describing how the labor market does not function very well in the absence of public intervention. The market alone provides neither the information needed to quickly match job-seekers with jobs nor the incentives needed to ensure an adequate investment in worker training. Both the flexible use of labor within the firm and the mobility of workers within the external labor market depend upon general educational skills. Yet without public supports and constraints, individuals and firms cannot be sure of realizing a return on their training investment, and the general skill level of the work force will remain too low. In short, without an effective employment and training system the labor market generates neither the information nor the human capital needed to maintain a high living standard.

The counterargument to laissez-faire begins with the failure of unregulated markets to produce good information and adequate training, but it also emphasizes the benefits of employment stability and security. Judged against the ideal of a self-regulating market, unemployment insurance and job protection measures produce less efficient outcomes. In the real world, markets operate under numerous social and political constraints, and the benefits of social programs and regulations can easily outweigh their costs. Unemployment compensation subsidizes longer jobless spells, but it also promotes better job matches. And by sustaining the confidence and buying power of the unemployed, it helps to prevent the sharp downturns in consumer spending that deepen recessions and slow economic recoveries. Job security provisions raise dismissal costs and slow the adjustment of employment to changes in demand, but employment protections also lessen resistance to technological and organizational change and motivate workers to learn specific skills.

Public policies and programs do not act in isolation, and the costs and benefits of specific interventions need to be analyzed within the overall context in which they operate. Even when the effects of a social program are negative, they can be minimized or offset by other interventions. The adverse effects of job protection measures can be minimized by means of subsidies that lower the costs of working short-time. To argue that the loss of labor market flexibility due to job security provisions always outweighs the benefits of stable employment relationships assumes that laying off or dismissing workers is the only way to adjust to changes in labor demand. In fact, it is just as easy to reduce the average number of hours worked. By encouraging employers to rely upon alternative forms of labor market adjustment, public policy can promote both flexible staffing and increased job security.

This concluding chapter discusses the possibilities of work sharing, both as an alternative to temporary layoffs and as a general strategy for combating unemployment. Work sharing provides an alternative to temporary layoffs by enabling firms to reduce the number of hours worked rather than the number of persons employed, and the following section describes how several European countries subsidize this alternative by offering short-time compensation through their unemployment insurance systems. The combination of job protections and the availability of short-time compensation gives employers an incentive to adjust to temporary or cyclical declines in sales by shortening the average workweek, rather than by laying off workers.

Work sharing can also be used to combat long-term unemployment. Proposals for reducing the length of the workweek or the workyear in order to create additional jobs have generated widespread interest and debate in Europe. They have attracted less support in this country even though we work roughly one month a year more than the Germans, French, and most other Europeans. In recent years the need for work sharing has been evidenced by a widening disparity in the opportunities for full-time employment. The length of the average workyear has increased, and the proportion of the work force that is under- or unemployed has grown as well. Like worker earnings, the hours of employment are polarizing. Millions of people have difficulty finding attractive, full-time jobs, while an even greater number feel compelled to work well beyond the standard workweek. There may be little chance at present of legislating a shorter workweek, but voluntary work-sharing arrangements offer the long-term possibility of increasing the number of attractive jobs and raising the level of social welfare.

WORK SHARING AS AN ALTERNATIVE TO TEMPORARY LAYOFFS

As concern over worker displacement increased over the past decade, there were attempts to limit the use of layoffs. A growing number of collective-bargaining agreements included job security provisions, and in 1988 Congress passed the Worker Adjustment and Retraining Notification Act (WARN). WARN requires companies to give at least sixty days notice in cases of dismissals that affect one-third of the work force at a given site within a thirty-day period. Prior to the passage of WARN, most U.S. companies gave little or no warning of layoffs to their employees.[2]

Admittedly, collective bargaining agreements cover a small and decreasing portion of the work force and WARN, although a major precedent, is a weak deterrent to layoffs and dismissals. The threshold that triggers the notification requirement—that at least one-third of the work force at a site be dismissed within a thirty-day period—is set too high. That threshold and other loopholes in the law allow employers to circumvent the legislation's intent. For example, employers who can show that layoffs are due to "unforeseen business circumstances" are not required to give advance notice. WARN also has no provision for compensating those displaced. The only financial penalty for layoffs that most employers face is an increase in their UI tax liability. The UI tax in this country is experience rated, which means that the payroll tax rate increases with the number of layoffs. The magnitude of this tax liability varies, but it is estimated to average about three weeks' wages for each worker laid off, up to a maximum rate.[3] Once an employer is paying the maximum tax rate, there is no penalty for laying off additional workers.

The sanctions that employers face in most European countries in cases of dismissal are much stronger. Legal provisions vary from one country to another, but workers usually have the right to advance notice and to severance pay or other compensation. Economists Katherine Abraham and Susan Houseman (1993, 1994) describe some of these job protection provisions in a cross-national study of labor market adjustment that compares the United States to several European countries. In Germany, for instance, there is no such thing as a temporary layoff. Workers who are dismissed have no recall rights and lose any company benefits to which they were entitled, but their dismissal must be socially justified. Germany's industrial relations system provides for works councils that share responsibility for the shop floor governance of all but the smallest establishments, and these works councils must receive at least thirty days notice of any collective dismissal. Dismissals are considered justified only if workers cannot be transferred elsewhere in the company, and only if the company has exhausted the alternatives to layoff, such as eliminating all overtime. In what is generally regarded as the most important provision in Germany's collective dismissal law, the Works Constitution Act of 1973 requires most companies to negotiate with the works councils on compensation for workers affected by collective dismissals. No severance payment is required in layoffs that are not collective dismissals, but for those that are the payment is substantial. Between 1980 and 1985, the median settlement for blue-collar workers under this provision of the Works Constitution Act amounted to approximately seventeen weeks' pay.[4] This financial penalty is nearly six times as large as the UI tax liability that U.S. employers incur. Layoffs are not bargained with works councils in other European countries, but companies are usually required to give advance notice and to make severance payments or other compensation in cases of collective dismissals.

Advance notice and severance pay requirements raise the cost of dismissals and can be expected to slow the adjustment of employment to changes in output. Less flexible staffing, in turn, discourages employers from taking on new hires and may lead to higher unemployment over the business cycle. But this logic assumes that job protection measures operate in isolation when, in fact, many European countries compensate for raising the cost of dismissals by lowering the cost of alternative forms of adjustment. They encourage employers to use work sharing as an alternative to layoffs by offering short-time compensation through their UI systems. Under these compensation schemes, employees whose workweek is reduced to four days instead of the usual five would receive 80 percent of their usual pay from their employer plus 20 percent of the unemployment benefits to which they are entitled. Because the UI tax is not experience rated, employers are not penalized for using short-time. Thus while advance notice and severance pay requirements make layoffs more costly, subsidizing the use of short-time through the UI system makes the alternative of work sharing less costly.

Together, job protection measures and the availability of short-time compensation give employers an incentive to adjust to economic downturns by reducing the average number of hours worked rather than by laying people off. European manufacturers are slower to reduce employment when faced with a decline in sales, but the speed with which they adjust their labor input is comparable to that of U.S. manufacturers (Abraham and Houseman 1993:72–73). Instead of immediately resorting to layoffs, they reduce the total hours worked through work sharing. Over the longer term, they rely upon attrition, job buyouts, and early retirement to adjust to a decline in sales. Because the government subsidizes short-time work, these employers have an incentive to avoid layoffs, and their success in doing so indicates that greater job security is compatible with employment flexibility.

As alternative forms of labor force adjustment, work sharing and temporary layoffs are functional substitutes, but their consequences for employers and workers differ considerably. Temporary layoffs are more disruptive of work routines and workplace organization. Layoffs also increase the risk that valued employees will take other jobs and that employers will eventually incur the costs of hiring and training replacements. Over the duration of a thirteen-week period, approximately 25 percent of American workers who are laid off take new jobs. During layoffs that last twenty-six weeks, roughly 40 percent find other jobs (Abraham and Houseman 1993:93). In addition, for those who are not recalled, layoffs result in longer unemployment spells than plant closings or dismissals because people often wait before beginning active search. Finally, layoffs are less equitable than work sharing. The impact of a layoff falls upon a fraction of the work force, while reducing the average number of hours worked spreads that impact more evenly across the work force.

The United States is unique among advanced industrial countries in the extent to which companies lay off or dismiss workers. The laws governing dismissals are weak, and there are no legal restrictions on laying off workers for economic reasons. Nor do we subsidize short-time work. Some states currently offer short-time compensation that allows employees whose hours are cut back to draw unemployment benefits proportional to the part of the week that they do not work, but these programs have not been widely used because short-time compensation, like regular unemployment benefits, is financed through an experience-rated tax that increases with program use. The fixed cost of fringe benefits, and especially of health insurance, is also a disincentive to the use of short-time work. By temporarily laying workers off during economic downturns, companies often avoid the fringe benefit expenditures that they would be obligated to pay for employees on short-time. Workers on layoff usually pay their own medical expenses, or third parties assume the payments when the unemployed and their families are forced to seek emergency care.

To make work sharing an attractive alternative to temporary layoffs, we need to raise the costs of laying workers off while reducing the costs associated with short-time work. We could begin by applying the advance notification provisions of WARN to temporary layoffs, and by lowering the threshold that triggers this notification requirement. Companies could also be required to extend health insurance coverage to workers on layoff and to make severance payments based upon years of service in cases of dismissal.

These job protection measures will result in employers hiring fewer full-time workers when business conditions improve unless the costs of short-time work are reduced at the same time. Abraham and Houseman (1993:141–45) recommend that every state be required to offer partial unemployment compensation to workers, and that this short-time compensation be funded through general tax revenues or through a payroll tax that is not experience rated. The cost to employers of providing health insurance and other fringe benefits when hours are reduced could also be at least partially subsidized. Together, these measures would reverse the prolayoff bias of the current UI system. Whatever the specific initiatives adopted, their purpose should be to stabilize the employment relationship. They should make it less costly to reduce the average number of hours worked, and more costly to reduce the number of people employed, when companies are forced to adjust to temporary downturns.

WORK SHARING AS A MEANS OF JOB CREATION

Short-time work stabilizes employment within the firm by providing an alternative to temporary layoffs, and it extends the period over which permanent work force reductions take place, allowing time for attrition to minimize the impact of displacement. Work sharing can also be used to create jobs and not just to prevent or slow their loss. A more proactive approach to work sharing seeks to combat unemployment by shortening the workweek or the workyear of those who are employed.

As the introductory quote from Juliet Schor's *The Overworked American* points out, it is one of the ironies of our national economic life that increased work time for the majority has accompanied the enforced idleness of a growing minority. Between 1969 and 1987 the length of the paid workyear increased by 305 hours for the typical female worker and by 98 hours for the typical male. Over the same time period the proportion of the work force that was either unemployed or had to accept involuntary part-time or part-year employment more than doubled, rising from 7 to nearly 17 percent (Schor 1992:29, 40). These divergent trends reveal the extent to which employment opportunities have polarized. While a growing number of people cannot find full-time jobs, an even greater number feel compelled to work ever longer hours. Reversing these trends will entail a change in outlook on the part of both employers and workers, and a public appreciation of the possibilities of work sharing.

The idea of creating more jobs by working fewer hours has a long lineage. As early as 1887 Samuel Gompers declared, "As long as we have one person seeking work who cannot find it, the hours of work are too long" (cited in Best 1990:236). During the depression many companies tried to prevent layoffs by cutting back on the hours of work. This forced workers to accept large pay cuts without compensation and soon became unpopular, but other work-limiting initiatives found greater acceptance. The legislation that created Social Security and removed millions of workers from the labor market by providing retirement income won wide support and remains the centerpiece of our social welfare system. The Fair Labor Standards Act of 1938 was another successful work sharing initiative. It limited the standard work week to forty hours and required time-and-a-half payment for overtime. Recent efforts to limit the use of overtime further by raising the wage rate to double-time have not been successful, although the idea of work sharing has been advanced by collective bargaining agreements that reduce the length of the workweek, permit early retirement, or allow for sabbaticals.

Today, the most ambitious efforts to increase employment by restricting the hours of work are being made in Europe. Germans already work a thirty-seven-hour week with six weeks of vacation, the shortest hours among industrial nations. In France the so-called Larrouturou proposal (named after its civil servant author) calls for the creation of two million additional jobs by switching from a five-day, thirty-nine-hour week to a four-day, thirty-three-hour week. Under this proposal, the cost to companies from the reduction in the average number of hours worked would be offset by productivity gains, a 5 percent pay cut, and the elimination of the 8.8 percent payroll tax that funds unemployment insurance. If realized, these savings would make the proposed change cost neutral. Its budgetary impact would depend upon the actual number of jobs created. Eliminating the payroll tax would result in a huge drain on public revenues, but two million fewer unemployed would save the government even more in income support payments (Cohen 1993).

This proposed reduction in the length of the French workweek could expand the job base and reduce unemployment without greatly reducing wages or undermining social welfare programs, but it is likely to have consequences that are not fully anticipated by many of its supporters. The appeal of any work-sharing proposal for employers lies in the kind of flexibility that it confers over the hours and organization of work. Much of the support for the four-day week in France is coming from managers and politicians who view it as a quid pro quo for more flexible work shifts that would allow machinery to operate for longer periods. Some of the companies that have already moved to a four-day week also instituted night and weekend work without overtime.[5] Whether exchanging normal working hours and the possibility of overtime pay for a shorter workweek accords with the preferences of most workers is not clear. Nor is it apparent that the reduction in the average workweek at these companies has generated an equivalent number of new jobs. The productivity gains from running machinery around the clock not only offset the cost of hiring additional workers, they eliminate the need for many of those workers as well.

Proposals for reducing the length of the standard workweek have attracted less support in this country than in Europe. An alternative approach that might build support for work-sharing proposals would eliminate compulsory overtime and allow voluntary work time reductions. The use of overtime in this country has risen to unprecedented levels. By 1993 the overtime put in by U.S. manufacturing workers had reached an average of 4.3 hours a week, the highest on record (Cohen 1993). Behind this trend is an incentive structure that fosters a reliance upon overtime at one end of the employment spectrum and the use of involuntary part-time workers at the other. The way in which fringe benefits are usually provided is a disincentive to hiring additional full-time workers. Fringe benefits such as pensions and health insurance are normally paid on a per person basis, so employer contributions for those receiving benefits do not vary with the number of hours worked. This fixed labor expenditure creates a powerful bias against additional hiring and in favor of overtime, and this bias has grown stronger as the fringe benefit share of total compensation increases. Surveys conducted by the U.S. Chamber of Commerce indicate that the share of fringe benefits in total compensation rose from 28 percent in 1969 to 37 percent in 1988 (Tilly 1991:13).

The employment practices of some of our major corporations show how this growing fringe benefits expenditure is linked to the use of overtime and to potential job losses. In the early 1980s as the economy came out of recession, the top management of USX (formerly U.S. Steel) issued a directive to plant managers ordering them to use overtime to avoid calling back laid-off workers and reentitling them to benefits. This use of overtime resulted in the loss of ten thousand potential jobs throughout the steel industry. Similarly, the United Autoworkers Union calculated in 1988 that overtime in the auto industry represented a loss of eighty-eight thousand potential jobs (Schor 1992:67–68). The fixed costs of health insurance and other benefits also contribute to the growing reliance upon temporary and involuntary part-time workers, who receive few if any benefits. Any attempt to eliminate overtime and reduce the length of the average workweek without at the same time reducing the fringe benefits expenditure will face strong employer opposition. If they are to result in a proportionate number of new full-time jobs, voluntary forms of work sharing will have to allow for more variable labor costs.

Even in the absence of the fixed cost of fringe benefits, any attempt to alter overtime practices will encounter resistance from employers and from many employees. Most employers regard the movement toward a more open world economy as a competitive challenge that is forcing us to work longer as well as harder. Schor illustrates the pervasiveness of this viewpoint by describing the responses of three hundred business leaders to a letter advocating a shorter workweek. Not a single response was favorable. The reply from the chief executive officer of a Fortune 500 company was typical:

My view of the world, our country and our country's needs is diametrically opposite of yours. I cannot imagine a shorter work week. I can imagine a longer one both in school and at work if America is to be competitive in the first half of the next century. (1992:152)

Although widely held, the belief that working longer hours makes us more competitive is wrong. What matters is not how many hours individuals work but how productively they work them. In most of the major industrial countries people work less than we do. Their goods are competitive in international markets because they produce them in fewer hours, not because individual workers spend more time on the job. It is true that the Japanese work longer hours than American workers. It is also true that the length of their working day has been shown to lower productivity, and *karoshi*, or death by overwork, has become a public concern in Japan. So much so that the Japanese government has made a workyear of eighteen hundred hours a national goal, which, if achieved, means that they too will work less than we do (Schor 1992:154).

The pressure to work longer hours is not confined to employers facing international competition. It also comes from the falling real wages and slow income growth that affect millions of families. For most workers, the main drawback to work sharing is the perception that it will threaten their living standards. They regard overtime as their only means of providing a more comfortable living for their families. Unfortunately, proposals that call for wage cuts to offset all or part of a reduction in the number of hours worked only reinforce this perception. The way to change this outlook is to link reduced work time to productivity gains, not to wage cuts. One promising proposal would allow workers to exchange all or part of the wage increases from future productivity gains for a shorter workweek or longer vacations. Voluntary arrangements that enable people to reduce gradually the length of the workyear without lowering their real earnings strengthen job attachment and motivation, while creating a better understanding of the possibilities of work sharing. Over time, even a voluntary program could substantially reduce the average annual hours of work. If only one-third of the slow economic growth projections of the BLS were exchanged for leisure, the length of the average workyear would have dropped from 1,911 hours in 1976 to 1,598 hours by the year 2000 (Best 1990:249).

Voluntary exchanges of future income for free time will not solve the problems of worker displacement and unemployment, but work-sharing arrangements that link the length of the workyear to productivity gains refute the belief that working longer means working better. Furthermore, as long as the programs are voluntary, they help to ensure that the length of the workweek reflects the shared preferences of workers and employers. It is in the interest of employers to be able to institute work time arrangements that result in a more flexible and productive work force. It is in the interest of workers to be able to choose to work fewer or more flexible hours without jeopardizing their living standards. Voluntary reductions in work time are one way to reconcile those interests.

In the end, the debate over work sharing is important because it raises fundamental questions about how and why we work. If our goal is to provide a better way of life, then work must be a collective undertaking. It must not only increase the amount of goods and services we produce, but also reinforce the bonds that link us together and to the larger society. One of the ways in which work contributes to the general welfare is by reminding us of our interdependence and by providing us with a sense of common purpose. Work sharing alone will not meet the need for more and better jobs, but the possibility of working shorter hours without any loss of real income provides an alternative to policies that are creating an increasingly insecure and disposable work force.

NOTES

1.   At the end of 1993, the unemployment rate in the twelve-nation European Community stood at 11.3 percent, with more than nineteen million people out of work (Cohen 1993:A1).

2.   A study by the General Accounting Office found that 30 percent of the businesses experiencing mass layoffs during the years 1983 and 1984 gave no warning to their blue-collar workers, and 26 percent gave no notice to white-collar workers. Roughly an additional third gave two weeks' notice or less (Abraham and Houseman 1993:34–35).

3.   Abraham and Houseman (1993:37) derive this estimate based upon the amount of weekly benefits (about 35 percent of wages), upon the average duration of benefits over the business cycle (about fourteen weeks), and upon the share of benefits for which the employer pays through higher taxes (about 60 percent).

4.   One study cited by Abraham and Houseman (1993:38) found that in 1978 German employers made severance payments in about one-third of all dismissals.

5.   For example, BMW and Hewlett-Packard instituted night and weekend work at their French plants following the shift to a four-day week (Cohen 1993:A6).

References _____

Abraham, Katherine G. and Susan N. Houseman. 1993. *Job Security in America: Lessons from Germany.* Washington, DC: Brookings Institution.

————. 1994. "Does Employment Protection Inhibit Labor Market Flexibility? Lessons from Germany, France, and Belgium." Pp. 59–93 in *Social Protection versus Economic Flexibility,* edited by Rebecca M. Blank. Chicago: University of Chicago Press.

Amondson, Norman E. and W. A. Borgen. 1982. "The Dynamics of Unemployment: Job Loss and Job Search." *Personnel and Guidance Journal* 60(May):562–64.

Anderson, Patricia, Walter Corson, and Paul Decker. 1990. *The New Jersey Unemployment Insurance Reemployment Demonstration Project: Follow-Up Report.* Washington, DC: U.S. Department of Labor.

Aschauer, David A. 1989. "Is Public Expenditure Productive?" *Journal of Monetary Economics* 23(March):177–200.

Baily, Martin Neal and Alok K. Chakrabarti. 1988. *Innovation and the Productivity Crisis.* Washington, DC: Brookings Institution.

Bakke, E. Wright. 1933. *The Unemployed Man.* London: Nisbet.

Barnet, Richard J. 1993. "The End of Jobs." *Harper's Magazine* (September):47–52.

Barnow, Burt S. 1987. "The Impact of CETA Programs on Earnings: A Review of the Literature." *Journal of Human Resources* 18:539–56.

Bartik, Timothy J. 1990. *Who Benefits from State and Local Economic Development Policies?* Kalamazoo, MI: W.E. Upjohn.

Bartlett, Donald L. and James B. Steele. 1992. *America: What Went Wrong?* Kansas City: Andrews and McNeel.

Bassi, Laurie J. 1994. "Workplace Education for Hourly Workers." *Journal of Policy Analysis and Management* 13(Winter):55–74.

Becker, Gary S. 1975. *Human Capital: A Theoretical and Empirical Analysis, with Special Reference to Education,* 2nd edition. New York: Columbia University Press.

Bensman, David and Roberta Lynch. 1988. *Rusted Dreams: Hard Times in a Steel Community.* Berkeley: University of California Press.

Benton, Lauren, Thomas R. Bailey, Thierry Noyelle, and Thomas M. Stanback, Jr. 1991. *Employee Training and U.S. Competitiveness.* Boulder: Westview.

Best, Fred J. 1990. "Work Sharing: An Underused Policy for Combating Unemployment." Pp. 235–57 in *The Nature of Work,* edited by Kai Erikson and S. P. Vallas. New Haven, CT: Yale University Press.

Blank, Rebecca M. and Richard B. Freeman. 1994. "Evaluating the Connection Between Social Protection and Economic Flexibility." Pp. 21–41 in *Social Pro-*

tection versus Economic Flexibility: Is There a Trade-Off? edited by Rebecca M. Blank. Chicago: University of Chicago Press.

Bluestone, Barry and Irving Bluestone. 1992. *Negotiating the Future: A Labor Perspective on American Business.* New York: Basic Books.

Browne, Lynn E. 1985. "Structural Change and Dislocated Workers." *New England Economic Review* (January–February):15–30.

Calleo, David P. 1992. *The Bankrupting of America: How the Federal Budget Is Impoverishing the Nation.* New York: William Morrow.

Castro, Janice. 1993. "Disposable Workers." *Time* (March 29):43–47.

Cobb, Sidney and Stanislav Kasl. 1977. *Termination: The Consequences of Job Loss.* Washington, DC: National Institute of Occupational Health and Safety.

Cohen, Roger. 1993. "Europeans Consider Shortening Workweek to Relieve Joblessness." *New York Times,* December 22.

Cohen, Stephen S. and John Zysman. 1987. *Manufacturing Matters: The Myth of the Post-Industrial Economy.* New York: Basic Books.

Commission on the Skills of the American Work Force. 1990. *America's Choice: High Skills or Low Wages.* Rochester, NY: National Center on Education and the Economy.

Congressional Budget Office. 1982. *CETA Training Programs—Do They Work for Adults?* Washington, DC: U.S. Government Printing Office.

Council of Economic Advisors. 1985. *The Annual Report of the Council of Economic Advisors.* Washington, DC: U.S. Government Printing Office.

———. 1988. *Economic Report of the President.* Washington, DC: U.S. Government Printing Office.

———. 1993. *Economic Report of the President.* Washington, DC: U.S. Government Printing Office.

Dean, Edwin and Kent Kunze. 1988. "Recent Changes in the Growth of U.S. Multifactor Productivity." *Monthly Labor Review* 111(May):14–22.

Denison, Edward F. 1985. *Trends in American Economic Growth, 1929–1982.* Washington, DC: Brookings Institution.

Dertouzos, Michael L., Richard K. Lester, and Robert M. Solow. 1989. *Made In America: Regaining the Productive Edge.* Cambridge, MA: MIT Press.

Devine, Joel A. and James D. Wright. 1993. *The Greatest of Evils: Urban Poverty and the American Underclass.* Hawthorne, NY: Aldine de Gruyter.

Dickens, William and Lawrence Katz. 1987. "Inter-industry Wage Differences and Industry Characteristics." Pp. 48–89 in *Unemployment and the Structure of Labor Markets,* edited by Kevin Lang and Jonathan Leonard. Oxford: Blackwell.

Doeringer, Peter B., Kathleen Christensen, Patricia M. Flynn, Douglas T. Hall, Harry C. Katz, Jeffrey H. Keefe, Christopher J. Ruhm, Andrew M. Sum, and Michael Useem. 1991. *Turbulence in the American Workplace.* New York: Oxford University Press.

Doyle, Philip M. 1985. "Area Wage Surveys Shed Light on Decline in Unionization." *Monthly Labor Review* 108(September):13–20.

Drucker, Peter F. 1993. *Post-Capitalist Society.* New York: HarperCollins.

Dudley, Kathryn M. 1994. *The End of the Line: Lost Jobs, New Lives in Postindustrial America.* Chicago: University of Chicago Press.

Economist. 1989. "Taking Care of Business." *Economist* (February 18):32.

Eisinger, Peter K. 1988. *The Rise of the Entrepreneurial State: State and Local Economic Development Policy in the United States.* Madison: University of Wisconsin Press.

Farber, Henry. 1993. "The Incidence and Costs of Job Loss: 1982–1991." Mimeo (March), Princeton University, Princeton, NJ.

Feldstein, Martin. 1973. "The Economics of the New Unemployment." *Public Interest* 33(Fall):3–42.

Flaim, Paul O. and Ellen Sehgal. 1985. "Displaced Workers of 1979–83: How Well Have They Fared?" *Displaced Workers, 1979–83.* Washington, DC: Bureau of Labor Statistics.

Freeman, Richard B. (ed.). 1994. *Working Under Different Rules.* New York: Russell Sage.

———. 1993. "How Much Has De-Unionization Contributed to the Rise in Male Earnings Inequality?" Pp. 133–63 in *Uneven Tides: Rising Inequality in America,* edited by Sheldon Danzinger and Peter Gottschalk. New York: Russell Sage.

Freeman, Richard B. and James L. Medoff. 1984. *What Do Unions Do?* New York: Basic Books.

Freud, Sigmund. [1930] 1963. *Civilization and Its Discontents.* London: Hogarth.

Friedman, Benjamin M. 1989. *Day of Reckoning: The Consequences of American Economic Policy.* New York: Vintage.

Gargan, Edward A. 1993. "India Among the Leaders in Software for Computers." *New York Times,* December 29.

Glass, Stephen. 1994. "Yes We Kenosha." *Policy Review* 70(Fall):80–83.

Greenhouse, Steven. 1993. "Clinton Seeks to Narrow a Growing Wage Gap." *New York Times,* December 13.

Grunwald, Joseph and Kenneth Flamm. 1985. *The Global Factory: Foreign Assembly in International Trade.* Washington, DC: Brookings Institution.

Gullickson, William and Michael J. Harper. 1987. "Multifactor Productivity in U.S. Manufacturing, 1949–83." *Monthly Labor Review* 110(October):18–27.

Hall, Robert. 1970. "Why Is the Unemployment Rate So High at Full Employment?" *Brookings Papers on Economic Activity* 3:369–402.

———. 1972. "Turnover in the Labor Force." *Brookings Papers on Economic Activity* 3:709–56.

Hamermesh, Daniel S. 1989. "What Do We Know about Worker Displacement in the U.S.?" *Industrial Relations* 28(Winter):51–60.

Hammonds, Keith H., Kevin Kelly, and Karen Thurston. 1994. "The New World of Work." *Business Week* (October 17):76–87.

Harrison, Bennett and Barry Bluestone. 1988. *The Great U-Turn: Corporate Restructuring and the Polarizing of America.* New York: Basic Books.

Holzer, Harry J. 1989. "The Spatial Mismatch Hypothesis: What Has the Evidence Shown?" Mimeo, Michigan State University, East Lansing.

Hotz, V. Joseph. 1992. "Designing an Evaluation of the Job Training Partnership Act." Pp. 76–114 in *Evaluating Welfare and Training Programs in the 1990s,* edited by Irwin Garfinkel and Charles Moskel. Cambridge, MA: Harvard University Press.

Hurst, Joe B. and John W. Shepard. 1986. "The Dynamics of Plant Closings: An Extended Emotional Roller Coaster Ride." *Journal of Counseling and Development* 64(February):401–5.

Jacobson, Louis, Robert LaLonde, and Daniel Sullivan. 1993. *The Costs of Worker Dislocation.* Kalamazoo, MI: W.E. Upjohn.

Jahoda, Marie. 1982. *Employment and Unemployment: A Social-Psychological Analysis.* New York: Cambridge University Press.

Jahoda, Marie, Paul F. Lazarsfeld, and Hans Zeisel. 1971. *Marienthel: The Sociography of an Unemployed Community.* Hawthorne, NY: Aldine de Gruyter–New York: Atherton.

Janoski, Thomas. 1990. *The Political Economy of Unemployment: Active Labor Market Policy in West Germany and the United States.* Berkeley: University of California Press.

Kain, John. 1968. "Housing Segregation, Negro Employment, and Metropolitan Decentralization." *Quarterly Journal of Economics* 82(May):175–97.

Katz, Lawrence F. and Kevin M. Murphy. 1992. "Changes in Relative Wages, 1963–1987: Supply and Demand Factors." *Quarterly Journal of Economics* 107(February):35–78.

Kelvin, Peter and Joanna E. Jarrett. 1985. *Unemployment: Its Social and Psychological Consequences.* New York: Cambridge University Press.

Kenosha News. 1990. "Boom County." *Kenosha News,* December 10 (Special Report).

Kilborn, Peter T. 1992. "Caterpillar's Trump Card." *New York Times,* April 16.

_____. 1993. "U.S. Says Its Training Effort Fails Displaced Job Seekers." *New York Times,* October 15.

Killingsworth, Charles C. 1966. "Structural Unemployment in the United States." Pp. 128–55 in *Employment Problems of Automation and Advanced Technology,* edited by Jack Steiber. New York: St. Martin's.

Kletzer, Lori G. 1989. "Returns to Seniority after Permanent Job Loss." *American Economic Review* 79(June):536–43.

_____. 1991. "Job Displacement, 1979–86: How Blacks Fared Relative to Whites." *Monthly Labor Review* 114(July):17–25.

Krugman, Paul. 1990. *The Age of Diminished Expectations: U.S. Economic Policy in the 1990s.* Cambridge, MA: MIT Press.

_____. 1994. "Competitiveness: A Dangerous Obsession." *Foreign Affairs* 73(March/April):28–44.

Labich, Kenneth. 1993. "The New Unemployed." *Fortune* (March 8):40–49.

Leonard, Jonathan S. 1987. "The Interaction of Residential Segregation and Employment Discrimination." *Journal of Urban Economics* 21:323–46.

Levitan, Sar A. and Frank Gallo. 1988. *A Second Chance: Training for Jobs.* Kalamazoo, MI: W.E. Upjohn.

Levy, Frank and Richard J. Murnane. 1992. "U.S. Earnings Levels and Earnings Inequality: A Review of Recent Trends and Proposed Explanations." *Journal of Economic Literature* 30(September):1333–81.

Lippmann, Steve and John McCall. 1976a. "The Economics of Job Search: A Survey, Part I." *Economic Inquiry* 14(June):155–89.

_____. 1976b. "The Economics of Job Search: A Survey, Part II." *Economic Inquiry* 14(September):347–68.

Logan, John R. and Harvey L. Molotch. 1987. *Urban Fortunes: The Political Economy of Place.* Berkeley: University of California Press.

Lynch, Lisa M. 1994. "Payoffs to Alternative Training Strategies at Work." Pp. 63–95 in *Working Under Different Rules*, edited by Richard B. Freeman. New York: Russell Sage.

Marshall, Ray. 1989. *Youth Employment, Education, and Training in Sweden*. Washington, DC: U.S. General Accounting Office.

Marshall, Ray and Marc Tucker. 1992. *Thinking for a Living: Education and the Wealth of Nations*. New York: Basic Books.

Marston, Stephen T. 1985. "Two Views of the Geographic Distribution of Unemployment." *Quarterly Journal of Economics* 100(February):57–79.

Massey, Douglas S. and Nancy A. Denton. 1993. *American Apartheid: Segregation and the Making of the Underclass*. Cambridge, MA: Harvard University Press.

Milwaukee Journal. 1988. "Take Chrysler to Court, Residents Say." *Milwaukee Journal*, February 19.

Mishel, Lawrence R. 1989. "The Late Great Debate on Deindustrialization." *Challenge* 32(January/February):35–43.

Moore, Thomas S. 1990. "The Nature and Unequal Incidence of Job Displacement Costs." *Social Problems* 37(May):230–42.

———. 1992. "Racial Differences in Post-Displacement Joblessness." *Social Science Quarterly* 73(September):674–89.

Moore, Thomas S. and Gregory D. Squires. 1991. "Two Tales of a City: Economic Restructuring and Uneven Development in a Former Company Town." *Journal of Urban Affairs* 13(June):159–73.

Morse, Nancy C. and Robert S. Weiss. 1955. "The Function and Meaning of Work." *American Sociological Review* 20(February):191–98.

Munnell, Alicia H. 1990. "Why Has Productivity Growth Declined? Productivity and Public Investment." *New England Economic Review* (January/February):3–22.

Murnane, Richard J. and Frank Levy. 1994. "Comment: Stimulating Employer-Provided General Training." *Journal of Policy Analysis and Management* 13(Winter):75–81.

Nasar, Sylvia. 1994. "Statistics Reveal Bulk of New Jobs Pay Over Average." *New York Times*, October 17.

National Commission on Excellence in Education. 1983. *A Nation at Risk: The Imperative for Educational Reform*. Washington, DC: U.S. Government Printing Office.

Newman, Katherine. 1988. *Falling from Grace: The Experience of Downward Mobility in the American Middle Class*. New York: Free Press.

Nussbaum, Bruce. 1992. "Downward Mobility: Corporate Castoffs Are Struggling Just to Stay in the Middle-Class." *Business Week* (March 23):56–63.

Office of Technology Assessment. 1986. *Technology and Structural Unemployment: Reemploying Displaced Adults*. Washington, DC: U.S. Government Printing Office.

Osterman, Paul. 1988. *Employment Futures: Reorganization, Dislocation, and Public Policy*. New York: Oxford University Press.

Osterman, Paul and Rosemary Batt. 1993. "Employer-Centered Training for International Competitiveness." *Journal of Policy Analysis and Management* 12(Summer):456–77.

Pappas, Greg. 1989. *The Magic City: Unemployment in a Working-Class Community.* Ithaca, NY: Cornell University Press.

Pearlin, Leonard I., E. G. Menaghan, M. A. Lieberman, and J. T. Mullin. 1981. "The Stress Process." *Journal of Health and Social Behavior* 22(December):337–56.

Perrucci, Carolyn C., Robert Perrucci, Dena B. Targ, and Harry R. Targ. 1988. *Plant Closings: International Context and Social Costs.* Hawthorne, NY: Aldine de Gruyter.

Piore, Michael and Charles Sabel. 1984. *The Second Industrial Divide.* New York: Basic Books.

Plunkert, Lois M. 1990. "The 1980's: A Decade of Job Growth and Industry Shifts." *Monthly Labor Review* 113(September):3–15.

Podgursky, Michael and Paul Swaim. 1987a. "Job Displacement Earnings Loss: Evidence from the Displaced Worker Survey." *Industrial and Labor Relations Review* 41(October):17–29.

———. 1987b. "Duration of Joblessness Following Displacement." *Industrial Relations* 26(Fall):213–26.

Racine Labor. 1988. "Jackson: We're Drawing the Battle Line Here in Kenosha." *Racine Labor* (February 5):1.

Reich, Robert B. 1991. *The Work of Nations.* New York: Vintage.

Rosow, Jerome M. and Robert Zager. 1988. *Training—The Competitive Edge: Introducing New Technologies into the Workplace.* San Francisco: Jossey-Bass.

Schor, Juliet B. 1992. *The Overworked American: The Unexpected Decline of Leisure.* New York: Basic Books.

Seitchik, Adam. 1991. "Who Are Displaced Workers?" Pp. 51–82 in *Job Displacement: Consequences and Implications for Policy,* edited by John T. Addison. Detroit: Wayne State University Press.

Sharma-Jenson, Geeta. 1993. "Bringing Chicago North to Wisconsin." *Milwaukee Journal,* July 11.

Soukup, Victoria. 1988. "Chrysler's Closing Hits United Way." *Milwaukee Sentinel,* December 23.

Streek, Wolfgang. 1993. "Training and the New Industrial Relations." Pp. 167–87 in *Economic Restructuring and Emerging Patterns of Industrial Relations,* edited by Stephen R. Sleigh. Kalamazoo, MI: W.E. Upjohn Institute.

Summers, Lawrence. 1990. *Understanding Unemployment.* Cambridge, MA: MIT Press.

Thaler, Richard H. 1989. "Interindustry Wage Differentials." *Journal of Economic Perspectives* 3(Spring):181–93.

Thurow, Lester. 1992. *Head to Head: The Coming Economic Battle Among Japan, Europe, and America.* New York: Warner Books.

Tilly, Chris. 1991. "Reasons for the Continuing Growth of Part-time Employment." *Monthly Labor Review* (March):10–17.

U.S. Bureau of the Census. 1994. *Statistical Abstract of the United States, 1994.* Washington, DC: U.S. Government Printing Office.

U.S. Department of Labor, Bureau of Labor Statistics. 1989. *Handbook of Labor Statistics.* Bulletin 2340 (August). Washington, DC: U.S. Government Printing Office.

U.S. International Trade Commission. 1986. "U.S Trade Related Employment: 1978–84." Pub. No. 1855. Washington, DC: USITC.

Uchitelle, Louis. 1992. "Pay of College Graduates Is Outpaced by Inflation." *New York Times,* May 14.

———. 1993a. "Use of Temporary Workers Is on Rise in Manufacturing." *New York Times,* July 6.

———. 1993b. "Newest Corporate Refugees: Self-Employed but Low-Paid." *New York Times,* November 15.

———. 1994. "Job Losses Don't Let Up Even as Hard Times Ease." *New York Times,* March 22.

Wachtel, Howard M. 1992. *Labor and the Economy,* 3rd edition. Fort Worth, TX: Dryden.

Ward, Jack. 1990. "Report of Activity in Chrysler Dislocated Worker Project." Memorandum (April 3). Kenosha, WI: Job Development Training Corporation.

Weiler, Paul. 1986. "Milestone or Tombstone: The Wagner Act at Fifty." *Harvard Journal on Legislation* 23:1–31.

White, Joseph B. 1988a. "Chrysler to Donate Wisconsin Profits to Fund for Workers from Closed Plant." *Wall Street Journal,* February 17.

———. 1988b. "Factory Towns Start to Fight Back Angrily When Firms Pull Out." *Wall Street Journal,* March 8.

Wisconsin Job Service. 1990. "Demographic Data for Laidoff Chrysler Workers." Unpublished data, Lakeshore District Job Service.

Index _____

SOCIAL INSTITUTIONS AND SOCIAL CHANGE

An Aldine de Gruyter Series of Texts and Monographs

EDITED BY

James D. Wright